Finnish Sauna

Design and Construction

Building Information Foundation RTS
Rakennustieto Publishing, Helsinki

The RT Information Files and the material of this book were compiled by the following experts:
Markku Aarnio – Erkki Helamaa – Taina Heikkilä – Heikki Hyytiäinen – Jukka Jaatinen –
Kalevi Karhapää – Kari Koskinen – Pekka Laaksonen – Kari Louhenkilpi – Seppo Tammiluoma –
Esa Vapaavuori – Irmeli Visanti – Risto Vuolle-Apiala – Ilkka Vuori – Erkki Äikäs

Rakennustieto
www.rakennustieto.fi
P.O. Box 1004, 00101 Helsinki
Finland
Phone: + 358 207 476 400

Cover photos: front cover: a sauna in Tuuliniemi, Sodankylä,
architect Olavi Koponen, photo Jussi Tiainen;
back cover: (top) the Thorsby Smoke Sauna, architect Marko Huttunen,
photo Mikko Mälkki; (middle) a yard sauna, architect Seppo Häkli,
photo Jussi Tiainen.
Translation from Finnish: Contemporary Finnish Saunas / Gekko Design
(Gareth Griffiths and Kristina Kölhi)
Graphic design: Mina Jokivirta
© Rakennustietosäätiö RTS | The Building Information Foundation RTS and
Rakennustieto Publishing
Publisher: Rakennustieto Publishing
Printers: Karisto Oy, Hämeenlinna
6th, revised edition, 2007
ISBN 978-951-682-856-8

Preface

The best sauna in the world? Where's it to be found and what's it like? Any Finn sitting in a sauna somewhere else than in Finland undoubtedly faces these questions. The long explanation that follows usually starts with a deep sigh and the disappointing statement that actually there is no definite answer. The best sauna is just as good as each individual person's own best experience. But we Finns would not be world-renowned experts in the matter if we could not immediately continue by providing a list of essential, even compulsory, conditions for achieving the perfect sauna. The qualified candidate should have a peaceful site by a lake with a view over the clear water, a wooden construction and an intimate scale, and there should be quietness, a beautiful sunset, a couple of good friends, soft steam, the smell of fresh birch leaves, as well as one hundred or so other features that create the balanced subtlety of the perfect sauna. On the other hand, this may simply be my own personal wish-fulfilment.

A second series of questions deals with the behaviour in a sauna. What do you do first? When do you wash or cool down? Is it healthy to sit in the hot steam more than twice in one session? Are there certain rituals you should follow? There are theories about precisely how long you should sit in the sauna and how hot and humid the sauna should be – but such theories are definitely not Finnish. Our national wisdom about the perfect sauna session is simple – take your time and do it in your own way, as long as it feels good.

If you are planning to build a sauna and you don't happen to have a Finn available, then this book will be really useful. The information it contains has been collected from the Building Information Files for architects and builders and represents the best know-how available in Finland. All the facts and principles are based on a long tradition of practical knowledge developed over generations and which in recent times has been continuously updated through the committee work of top professionals. The information provides the basis for a successful sauna project – though experienced sauna builders often have their own well kept secrets about how to make the perfect sauna experience even better.

Matti Rautiola
Professor, Director General
Building Information Foundation RTS

Contents

1. **Basic Information** 5
   The Sauna and the Finns 5
   The Historical Development of the Sauna ... 9

2. **The Planning and Design of a Sauna** ... 28
   General Remarks 28
   Concepts 28
   The Location of the Sauna and Related
   Functions 30
   Planning of Rooms and Space in Saunas ... 38
   Planning a Sauna for Use by Disabled
   Persons 45

3. **Planning the Components and
   Elements of a Sauna** 47
   General Remarks 47
   Thermal Insulation 47
   Water and Moisture Insulation 48
   Components and Building Elements 49
   The Roof 52
   Additional Components 54
   Linings and Cladding 55

4. **Platforms and Furnishings** 59
   General Remarks 59
   The Platforms 59
   Furnishings and Equipment 65

5. **Sauna Stoves** 69
   General Remarks 69
   Wood-fired Stoves 69

   Electrically Heated Sauna Stoves 73
   Other Stove Types 74
   Protective Measures 74
   Flues 76
   The Stove Stones 78
   The Heating of Wood-fired Stoves 78

6. **The Design of Heating, Plumbing,
   Ventilation and Electrical Installations
   for the Sauna** 80
   General Remarks 80
   Heating 81
   Water Supply and Drains 81
   Ventilation 82
   Lighting 86
   Electrical Installations 87
   Installing an Electric Stove and a
   Wood-fired Stove in the Same Sauna 89

7. **Smoke Saunas** 91
   General Remarks 91
   Constructing a Traditional Smoke Sauna .. 91
   Building a Modern Smoke Sauna 95
   The Smoke Stove 98
   Heating a Smoke Sauna 102

Contemporary Finnish Saunas 105
   A Yard Sauna 106
   The Sireenimäki Sauna 110
   The Thorsby Smoke Sauna 114

1. Basic Information

This chapter is on the importance of the sauna in the Finnish tradition, the development of saunas along with means of livelihood and various areas of vernacular architecture, and the basic features and properties of the Finnish sauna.

Pekka Laaksonen

The Sauna and the Finns

There are some 1.7 million saunas in Finland, all in active use. No one has estimated how many times Finns bathe in saunas yearly, but it can be easily assumed that there are several million occasions per year when Finns withdraw into the warmth of the sauna to seek physical and psychological refreshment.

The sauna is such an integral and characteristic part of everyday culture in Finland that we Finns find it hard to understand its special significance or uniqueness. For us, the sauna is more than just a place in which to bathe. It is the focal point of a range of customs, traditions and beliefs.

Although the origins of the sauna still remain obscure, we know that the Finno-Ugrian peoples have a long association with it. Finns can well be regarded as a sauna people, for here it has retained its position better than elsewhere, while adapting to changes in other areas of culture.

Finnish cultural historians have demonstrated far-off parallels to our sauna and its special features. The Finnish type of sauna, in which water is thrown onto hot stones, combines the best of the hot-air and steam bath traditions.

One of the earliest documentary sources on the existence of the Finnish sauna is a description by the historian Nestor of Kiev in his famous chronicle from 1112. Nestor tells of hot wooden saunas, in which naked bathers beat themselves with branches and finally pour cold water over themselves. "Without any coercion they torture themselves and in this way gain pain instead of cleanliness", tells the chronicle. It has been romantically assumed that this description, relating to areas to the north of ancient Novgorod, referred to the sauna customs of the forefathers of the Finns.

Studies in architectural history around the turn of the century attempted to outline the chronological relationships of different types vernacular buildings and to place them within a "typological" system of development. It was claimed that the first stage in such an evolutionary chain was the underground sauna, dug into an embankment of sandy soil. It was assumed to have been the first permanent dwelling erected by slash-and-burn farmers when they moved into new areas.

This suggestion found support in the etymology of the word sauna, common to all the Baltic-Finnic languages. It was regarded as a derivative of savu, meaning "smoke". Accordingly, rising smoke would be the only visible sign of a dwelling built into a pit in the ground. The dwelling was literally "in smoke" (Fi. savuna), from which the word sauna was thought to derive.

When the Finns learned to master the technique of corner-joined log construction, the sauna could be built above the ground. At the same time, the word pirtti (cabin) appeared in the Finnish language. In some dialects it is used as a synonym for sauna. The evolutionary concept also suggested that dwelling cabins were first used as saunas and threshing sheds, like the sauna in Impivaara in Aleksis Kivi's novel Seven Brothers. Today, experts feel that the threshing shed and the sauna have a long history as separate buildings.

Researchers, however, maintained for many years that the sauna had close links with an agricultural economy throughout broad areas of Northeast Europe. It was suggested that bathing in the sauna was necessary after the sooty work in the threshing sheds and burn-cleared plots and fields. On the other hand, hunters and fishers had no similar need for sweating and washing in this manner.

Later studies have questioned the connection of the sauna with agriculture alone. It has been pointed out that the common feature of sauna cultures in different parts of the world is not bathing but perspiring, which would originally have had a ritual or healing purpose. Depending on the level of culture, the bathers sweated in tents, hide-covered teepees, earth-pit constructions, or log saunas.

Fig. 1. An old sauna in the Muurame Sauna Museum. The estimated time of construction is the end of the 19th century.

A new perspective on the age and origin of the sauna was found when it was discovered that the word sakna, the Proto-Finnic form of "sauna", had a parallel in the old Saami (Lapp) language. In Saami, this term meant a pit dug into the snow, as for example by a willow grouse. Stone Age sites, in turn, have revealed large hearths or fireplaces, which could have been used for heating stones for a sauna-type bath. Accordingly, it can be suggested that even the prehistoric Finns may have been familiar with the sauna. They would have heated stones in a pit (i.e. a sauna), covered the pit with hides, thrown water on the stones, and beaten themselves with branches.

The history of the Finnish sauna largely involves the study of vernacular architecture. It has been demonstrated how primitive stone-laid hearths developed into sauna stoves that were increasingly easier to heat and use. The sauna developed from a pit construction into a corner-joined log house at ground level and finally into the electrically heated saunas of modern apartment buildings.

In different parts of Finland, the sauna, like any other feature of folk culture, developed according to specific needs and other reasons in slightly different ways with respect to its size, the location of the stove, the platforms, and other technical aspects. There is also regional variation in sauna-related customs and beliefs.

The sauna was the poor man's pharmacy, where the sick were healed and where most of the ancestors of the present-day Finns were born. It was the place where a woman giving birth could withdraw from the hustle and bustle of everyday concerns, and take shelter from the curses and envy of supernatural powers.

The sauna was a sacred place. It was there that a child was made a member of his or her community and the mother was purified to return to her everyday chores after childbirth. Since these were tasks forbidden to men, the birthing sauna can well be described as the seat or cradle of traditional women's culture in Finland.

The sauna was a most suitable place for curing a variety of ills. There, the healer could concentrate in peace. As there were many beliefs associated with the sauna, the patient was perhaps more attuned to the situation at hand. The survival of the Finnish "cupping" or blood-letting custom was made possible by the sauna.

But the many charms and spells of the sauna healers have been replaced by modern methods. Fortunately, they were recorded and we known of many spells to induce love or to cure a number of ills. The old spells and charms open a fascinating perspective on the psychology of the ancient Finns. Kristfried Ganander's Mythologia Fennica from the eighteenth century tells of Auteretar (literally Mist-Woman), the spirit of the sauna. Auteretar was the mother of Auterinen, the steam of the stones.

Although the present Finnish sauna may not be demonstrably a uniquely Finnish invention, the longevity of the tradition and its vividness have made it an important element of the Finnish identity. This is particularly evident among Finns and their descendants living abroad.

Few were able to take their saunas with them, but the idea of the sauna remained and the materials were almost universally available.

The Finnish ethnographer Samuli Paulaharju describes this phenomenon as follows:

"It is in the warmth of the sauna that the Finn

begins his worldly journey, and he will take the sauna with him wherever he goes. Even on the barren treeless shores of the Arctic Ocean a Finn will gather driftwood and build a small turf-roofed sauna with a stove of stones from the shore, and will heat it with sod. He will throw water from fell streams on the stones and beat his back with a whisk of willow."

A number of popular Finnish sayings concerning the sauna offer an interesting picture of the beliefs, ideas and customs relating to the use of the sauna. One saying, for example, notes that if the sauna, spirits and tar won't help, then the patient must surely die. Another describes the sauna as the poor man's hospital, yet another compares it to a church etc.

Fig. 2. Underground sauna from Valkjärvi, at present in the Sauna Museum of Muurame. Photo: Teemu Töyrylä.

Erkki Helamaa

The Historical Development of the Sauna

In Finland, the sauna has age-old traditions, but it is still a living part of our culture. The sauna has faithfully followed Finns wherever they go, and its various stages are closely linked with changes in habitation and the way of life. Although much of the ancient sauna tradition has survived up to the present, the sauna has changed over its long history, and today's sauna is a space that differs considerably from the saunas of the past. Fortunately, there are still several thousand flueless or smoke saunas in Finland, which preserve features of a building tradition thousands of years old.

Everyone who designs or builds a sauna forges a link in a long chain of tradition, although the respective ends of this chain may differ. But to make a new link fit at least the preceding one, and to keep the chain unbroken, the architect and the builder should know something of the past. We must therefore undertake a brief journey into the history of the sauna.

"These Finns,
what have they achieved?
At one time, they lived in an area half the size of Russia.
But did they found an empire?
No!
When trouble raised its head, they left, sailed over the Finnish Gulf to Finland, sought out a stand of birches
and built a sauna there."

These words by former President J.K. Paasikivi present a candid view of the early history of the Finns, much in keeping with his sharp comments on our later achievements.

But like President Paasikivi, many historians and archaeologists have come to the conclusion, perhaps expressed more cautiously, that even before arriving in Finland our forefathers had adopted the sauna from neighbouring peoples, and they brought the custom with them.

The Finnish sauna is thus at least almost two thousand years old, assuming that it arrived with the first Finnish settlers in the first century AD. It should be remembered, though, that the Finns came to the area of present-day Finland from afar; they were dispersed in their wanderings and their journey took a long time. Even the final migration was a matter of centuries.

But the origin of the sauna is not a simple problem. Archaeology suggests another possibility: that there were saunas here long before the Finns. They were perhaps not sauna buildings as such, but sweat baths of some kind, as among various indigenous peoples in different parts of the world.

Accordingly, we may ask why this could not have been possible among those who first came here? The Finnish archaeologist and ethnographer Sakari Pälsi suggested that it was only logical to assume that there were "protosaunas" providing warmth and cleanliness. Pälsi bases this suggestion on his own horror at the thought that people would have lived and worked hard in this barren country without the benefit of the sauna.

The prehistoric sauna

Even at the risk of giving free rein to one's imagination, it can be claimed that the initial stages of the sauna are to be found at Stone Age dwelling sites, or more precisely among the remains of excavated hearths and fireplaces. The fireplaces of Stone Age dwellings were often so-called pit hearths, round-bottomed pits usually under a metre in diameter and approximately 30 cm deep, with two or three layers of stones on the bottom.

But there were also exceptionally large pit hearths up to two metres in diameter. In some cases archaeologists have found charred material among the bottom layer of stones. Pälsi suggested that this was the remains of a subsequently charred insulating layer. The insulation would have permitted the hearth to retain heat long after the fire itself went out. With reference to this observation and the fact that the large pit hearths rarely appear together with traces of dwellings, Pälsi claimed that they were "sauna stoves" of some kind. After heating the stones, a tent, for example of poles and hides, could have been erected over them. Could it be that the modern-day tent saunas make unwitting use of millennia-old methods?

The Finnish archaeologist Ville Luho suggests further support for Pälsi's theory in the results of excavations at a Stone Age site in Honkilahti.

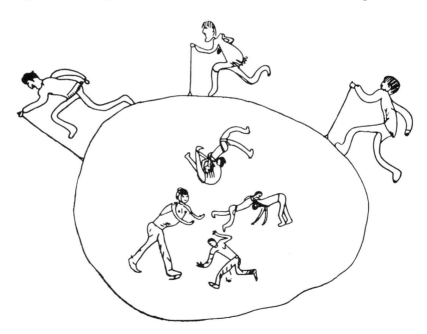

Fig. 3. A sweat bath does not always require a sauna. Drawing by Sakari Pälsi and Martti Santala showing a Chukchee "running bath". Skin under leather clothes requires perspiration and ventilation, which is why the Chukchee men go off for a run every now and then. They run, perspire and air themselves contentedly.

There, a depression in the shape of the bottom of a large vessel was found next to a large pit hearth. Could these have been the stove and the hot water container? Luho goes on to point out that this idea should not be taken too seriously. But in any case, the small pit or depression was a good place to store a large Stone Age pot with its round base, perhaps with hot water for the bath.

The original sauna

Emerging from the mists of prehistory, the sauna became part of the way of life wherever Finns settled. At first, it followed hunters and fishers from one site to another. As they could only carry the most essential equipment with them, their dwellings, and also their saunas, had to be temporary structures that were easy to erect. A conical hut, similar to a teepee, could have been suitable for this purpose.

The high conical form, however, was a poor design for a sauna, as the heat would rise to the top part. A lower hut of branches and withes would have been better, especially if it was partly sunk into the ground.

When a settled way of life evolved around burn-cleared plots in the wilderness, the mobility of dwellings ceased to be important. As there was now reason to expend more effort, the hut type sunk into a shallow depression in the ground became deeper. A floor in a deep depression suffered less from draught and was warmer than at ground level. There was reason to deepen the pit as its walls gave shelter from the wind and the frost, and finally the dwelling, except for its roof, was completely under ground level.

Like the later chimneyless cabin, this "underground cabin" was both a dwelling and a sauna. There is evidence of this in an early documentary source. Writing in the early tenth century, the Arabian traveller Ibn Dasta described a Slavonic tribe (whom the Finnish ethnologist U.T. Sirelius claimed were Mordvians), who lived during the winter in cellar-like dwellings sunk into the ground. They carried stones into their huts and heated them red-hot. Then they threw water on the stones, producing steam to heat the hut. And finally the dwellers took off their clothes.

Gradually, the pit dwelling came to be used only as a sauna. A great deal of information on this type of sauna has survived, and it can be described in considerable detail.

A pit approximately two metres square and two metres deep was dug in a bank of sandy soil. The walls could be of bare earth, but were most often lined with thin round logs, which in later times were split. When the log joining technique was mastered, two or three courses of logs could be laid to protect the upper part of the sauna from the elements. The sauna had a low two-faced, saddle-back roof with a layer of birch-bark and turf on top. In the summer, long grass would grow from the turf roof, camouflaging the whole sauna as a green grassy mound. In the winter, it was covered by the snow.

This original form had already developed the basic concept of the Finnish sauna: the stone-laid stove stood by the door to provide heat and on the rear or side wall next to the stove was a bench made of a split log, later replaced by a platform on posts.

The underground saunas remained in use for a long time. In the summers of 1907 and 1908

Fig. 4. An underground sauna belonging to the blacksmith Korhonen at Savikylä in Nurmes. Drawing by Samuli Paulaharju 1907–08. There is only bare earth in the lower part of the walls; the upper parts are of courses of logs. The floor is also bare earth. The roof is of boards, faced with birch bark and covered with earth. The platform is of two wide planks, with a third plank serving as a step and a seat. From *Karjalainen sauna* by Samuli Paulaharju.

the ethnographer Samuli Paulaharju saw a great number of these saunas during his expedition to Northern Karelia and the Dvina region further east. According to his observations, these were the saunas of the poor. As a log sauna could not be afforded, a pit was dug in the ground and little timber was needed. But despite this, the sauna when properly heated was said to serve the needs of its users well.

Underground saunas reappeared during the Second World War in front line conditions. Having to withstand enemy fire, they had to be built underground and the walls and ceiling had to be reinforced with sturdy logs. Travelling in Karelia in Eastern Finland in 1947 K.F. Hirvisalo saw completely new underground saunas, built during the post-war reconstruction effort. – Today, underground saunas are to be found only as reconstructions in museums, and perhaps in the private use of sauna enthusiasts.

The basic sauna

A fundamental change in building methods, also of saunas, occurred when the corner-joining of logs replaced the former upright hut constructions. The northern coniferous zone, beginning in Scandinavia and extending via Finland, Karelia and the Baltics to Russia and further via the tundra to Siberia, is one of the four areas on earth where corner-joining has been applied. The other three are the Alpine regions, North America and China.

Over the millennia saunas have extended from the Atlantic to the Pacific, across two continents, and their distribution has largely corresponded to the northern area of the corner-joining technique. It began in Finnmark on the Atlantic Coast - the Vikings having become acquainted with the sauna in Russia - and extended via North Sweden to Finland, Estonia and Karelia and further afield through Northern Russia and Siberia.

Various suggestions have been made concerning the adoption of corner-joining. With reference to a hut-floor excavated in Kaukola on the Karelian Isthmus, Sakari Pälsi assumes that Stone Age huts already had corner-joined lower courses of logs, as in present-day Lapp huts. U.T. Sirelius suggests an early date for the technique with reference to his own observation of little difference between a simple log-joint and a fence corner of horizontal timbers used in certain types of hunting traps. Despite this, he is not convinced that log-building techniques as such were known in Stone Age times, although some parts of structures, as also assumed by Pälsi, could have been made of logs. As is well known the joining technique also required developed bladed tools. The ethnologist Kustaa Vilkuna suggests the possibility that the ancient Finns were already familiar with corner-joining upon their arrival in Finland. He dates finds of clay used to caulk and seal gaps between logs to a period from the fourth to the eighth century AD. Lars Pettersson assumed that this technique probably came to Finland in the ninth century AD from the Russian-Byzantine culture – the same areas from where the sauna had come

For the settlers of the wilderness a small log building by a burn-cleared plot was a necessary 'multi-purpose facility", serving as a dwelling, a sauna, a threshing shed and even as a shelter for animals.

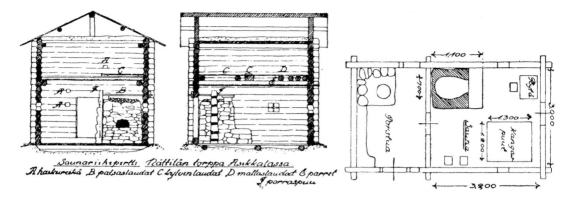

Fig. 5. A building serving three functions as a cabin, sauna and threshing shed. Rättilä tenant farm, Asikkala. Measured drawing by Veikko Kyander. From *Suomen kansanomaista kulttuuria* by U. T. Sirelius.

According to Aulis Ojajärvi and other experts, the combination of dwelling cabin, sauna and threshing shed is an old type of building, albeit temporary in most cases. When it became possible to erect separate buildings for various household needs, the sauna was also built separately. Some of the household chores were still carried out in the sauna. Ethnographers divide traditional Finnish saunas into three groups according to their size and layout. These groups do not have clearly limited areas of distribution. The East-Finnish sauna type originally covered an area comprising eastern Uusimaa, Karelia, Savo, Central Finland, and Northern Finland. The Häme-SW Finnish type (here known as the Häme type) was known in the regions of Häme, Satakunta, and so-called Finland Proper in the southwest. It also appears in western Uusimaa and South Ostrobothnia. The West-Finnish type had the most uniform and also the widest distribution, covering western Uusimaa, Finland Proper, Satakunta and Ostrobothnia.

Despite local differences, we may outline a picture of what can be called the "basic Finnish sauna, which in fact is still in use in almost original form. Today, it is known as the flueless or "smoke" sauna.

This was a simple four-cornered blockwork building of logs. The logs, stripped of bark and round in shape (hewn from the 17th century onwards) were laid and joined in horizontal courses. In the outer corners at the structurally important crossing of the logs different types of joins were used. The oldest and most simple join was made by carving a round notch in a log corresponding to the round form of the log to be laid upon it. Later, the round notches were carved on both sides of the log. The logs were allowed to project from the corners. As tools and implements developed, the joins achieved increasingly richer forms. The projecting logs crossing at the corners were cut to even lengths. The straight or flush corner which appeared in the late eighteenth century in dwellings and loft

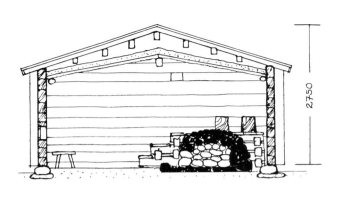
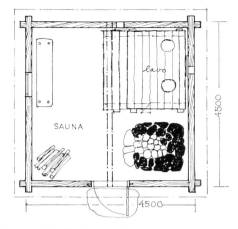

Fig. 6. The East-Finnish sauna (example here from Savo) was used primarily for bathing. In the sauna shown here (moved from Mikkeli Rural Commune to the Muurame Sauna Museum) the post-borne platform is against aside wall next to the stove. The floor plan and drawing are of the Miettinen sauna at Kaavi. Measured drawing by Risto Vuolle-Apiala. Muurame Sauna Museum. Photo: Teemu Töyrylä.

barns was rarely used in sauna construction.

Caulking the sauna walls was not a matter of great concern. If it was forgotten – or deliberately left out in the lowest courses – the sauna was better ventilated. Originally, clay daub was used to fill the gaps between the logs; moss tended to fall out from between the round surfaces. Later, when the logs were specially grooved to fit on top of each other, the moss caulking would remain in place.

Saunas were built to different size according to needs. The East-Finnish sauna, which was primarily for bathing, was relatively small, roughly three by three metres in area. Wall-plate level was some 2.5 metres from the ground, corresponding to 8–12 courses of logs. In North Finland there were saunas even under two metres in height.

The Häme type of sauna was used for a variety of household chores, primarily the preparation of malts and the drying of flax, which dictated the size and layout of the building. These saunas were large, up to six by six metres in floor area. In 1807 a sauna was built at Strandgård in Urjala with a floor area of some fifty square metres (12 x 11 ells). Thew Häme saunas were also high structures, at least over three metres but sometimes more than four. There had to be standing

BASIC INFORMATION | 15

room for a grown man under the shelf for the malts, and at least room to move on all fours at its sides.

The size of the West Finnish sauna varied according to the needs of the farm. In some places it was used only for bathing, but elsewhere it could serve a number of other purposes.

There was usually no porch or entrance room. The door was placed at one end of the building to prevent rainwater from the roof dripping on the bathers entering or leaving the sauna. Sometimes the coping at the end with the door was extended to form a long overhang, or, as in Central Finland, a structure of poles was built against the gable end or resting on a continuation of the ridge beam. In the large saunas of Häme, a log-built anteroom was a common feature at an early stage.

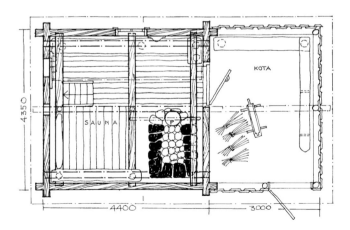

Fig. 7. The saunas of the Häme-SW Finnish type had shelves or platforms for preparing malts. The sauna in this picture (originally from Korpilahti now in the Muurame Sauna Museum) has a malt platform extending over the whole upper part with openings only for the stove and the bathers' platform. Measured drawing by Risto Vuolle-Apiala. Muurame Sauna Museum. Photo: Teemu Töyrylä.

The floor of the sauna was trodden earth or coarse sand and gravel. There could also be split logs laid on routes of access.

The roof was low-angled and two-faced and made of birch-bark with poles, which was followed by roofs of boarding and (in the late nineteenth century) shingles. When a separate ceiling was adopted, it was built on the interior roof supports. At first, the ceiling was of several faces and later of level form.

The stove was in the corner by the door. In East Finland, a small stove was sufficient; its lower part was of large rocks or slabs, followed by round stones, and finally by fist-sized stones on which the water was thrown.

In Häme the stove was quite large, up to two metres square and over a metre high. Preparing malts and curing meat made it necessary to maintain heat for long periods. The stove was rectangular; its regular exterior frame and sides were made of large, flat-surfaced stones or slabs. In the Satakunta region the stoves was made of brick, like the oven of the threshing sheds. The upper part of the stove was of large stones, and this part was borne by long supporting stones placed on top of the sides. The vault shape of the stove and the dome formed by the stones caused pressure against the sides, which required timber supports around the upper part of the masonry construction.

In southern parts of Western Finland the stove was fairly large and of regular shape, while in the northern areas it was a smaller and irregular construction of stones. A special feature was the location of the fire opening, towards the rear wall. Elsewhere, the fire opening faced the route from the door to the rear wall.

The platforms were often simple construc-

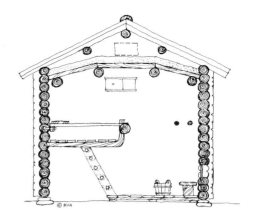

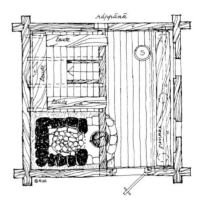

Fig. 8. In Central Finland and Satakunta there was a sauna type in which the bathers' platform was affixed to supports with curved stump-parts of tree trunks resembling sledge-runners. Measured drawing by Risto Vuolle-Apiala.

tions. Where they were placed high they had to be reached by a ladder. In the East-Finnish sauna the platform was supported by one or several posts and was placed against the side wall between the stove and the rear wall. There could be as many as four posts bracing the platform against the wall.

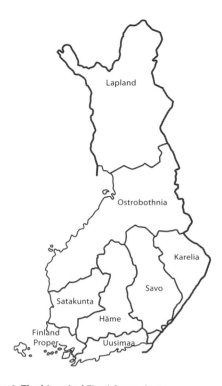

Fig. 9. The historical Finnish provinces.

bothnia, the rear-wall platform was supported by sturdy planks, whose ends projected from the side walls.

The sauna door was low ("only five courses high") and the threshold was high. There were a couple of ventilation holes with wooden shutters to serve as windows, let out smoke during the heating, and to provide ventilation during the actual bathing. When in later times, glass windows were fitted in the saunas, they were always placed low to remain clean and free of soot.

The ancient stoves without flues were gradually replaced by types with flues leading to a chimney. This was such a profound change that for a few decades the old smoke sauna was almost completely forgotten. It was to experience a renaissance at summer houses and cottages.

Saunas with flues

Hearths with flues had already appeared in the fifteenth century in manorial residences in Western Finland. By the seventeenth century, it had been adopted in larger farmhouses. In the early nineteenth century chimneys had become a common sight in the towns and the countryside in Southern and Western Finland. In the east and the north the last chimneyless cabins and cottages survived until the close of the nineteenth century. Around this time chimneys began to appear in various outbuildings, in which connection this innovation also influenced the sauna.

Following the "invention" of the original stove, the flue-equipped sauna stove was the first major change in the history of the Finnish sauna. It permitted the building of saunas in locations where the old flueless stoves could not be used.

In Central Finland a type of platform was developed which was supported by curved stumps. In Karelia and southern Savo platforms of corner-joined logs or beams were common.

The platform of the Häme sauna was largely similar to its counterparts in East Finland, but there was also a separate shelf for malts, which could also be used by the bathers. This structure occupied the whole upper part of the sauna room so that there were only openings at the stove and the other platforms. In the West-Finnish sauna the platform was in completely different location: at the rear wall with a transverse beam support in its front part. In Ostro-

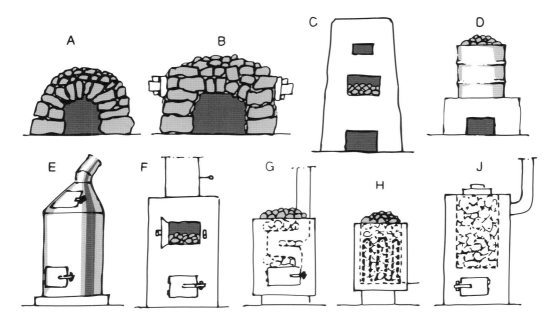

Fig. 10. The development of the sauna stove: A, Dome-shaped smoke stove of rocks and slabs from a small East-Finnish sauna; B, a stove from a large sauna in Häme with large stones or brick masonry in the lower part and a crossing member holding the structure together; C, late-nineteenth-century smoke stove encased in masonry; D, smoke stove made of a metal drum; E, flued heat-storage stove of sheet metal; F, flued stove of masonry; G, wood-fired continuous heating stove; H, continuous heating electric stove; J, heat-storage stove with thermal insulation. From *Rakennan saunan* by Pekka Tommila.

The sauna, however, acquired its flue in a roundabout way. At first, the large container for heating water was fitted with a flue and a chimney. The basic sauna type had developed into a version with an auxiliary room or entrance (of boarding or logs) on the side. This had replaced the earlier cooking hut adjacent to the sauna. In the entrance room was a large cast-iron container for heating water and other household chores.

Later, the sauna itself was fitted with a solid brick chimney. Today, sauna chimneys can be bought to required size from ironmongers. At first, the stove itself was made of brick, as in the chimneyless type in Satakunta. Now, it became a closed configuration, with a fire chamber in the lower part that could be closed with a shutter and a large space in the upper part with a lid that could be opened to emit heat after the stones had been heated. As the smoke could now be let out of the sauna, the builders wanted it to look clean, and the brick stove was often faced with smooth, white plaster.

In the 1920s a sheet-metal stove type came into use. These were originally home-made, but soon became a commercial article. The barrel-

 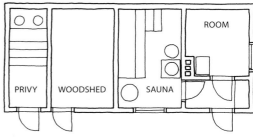

Fig. 11. The yard sauna of a single-family house.

Fig. 12. A yard sauna in Pispala, Tampere. Drawing by Erkki Helamaa.

shaped sheet-metal stoves were made in workshops and factories and were sold by iron- mongers. They are related to the former type in that they too have a closed fire chamber in the lower part and a lid to let out the heat in its conical upper part.

In its original heat-storage version, which is still in use, the flue stove is heated only once for the bathing. The smoke and combustion residues generated in the fire chamber with its grate are led via the heated stones to a flue. The heat for bathing depends on how much heat the stones have stored during the two or so hours required to heat the stove.

In the 1930s, a continuous heating stove model came into use. Here, the firewood burns in a separate chamber and the flames and smoke do not come into contact with the stones. The stove can thus provide heat as long as the fire is burning.

But which is better, the continuous heating type or the heat-storage model? This has been an eternal point of dispute and endless comparison. In both stove types the desired temperature is obtained by regulating the burning of the fuel. In the continuous heated type, the stones are not covered, whereby they dry the surrounding air, but heat the stove room in a short time. The heat-storage stove is slower, and a full comparison of the relative advantages and disadvantages will probably end in a draw.

The yard sauna

But in one respect the flue-equipped sauna was invaluable: it promoted the spread of saunas into the towns and cities. The old smoke sauna was a fire hazard in densely built areas. This was also true in rural conditions, as noted by the authorities. An act from 1681 stipulates that at tax-exempt and crown-owned holdings the sauna, owing to its potential fire hazards, could not be built in the yards of the farmstead but outside these areas. In 1734 it was officially laid down that the sauna and the threshing shed should be built apart.

By this time, however, the smoke sauna had already been adopted in the towns. Until the end of the nineteenth century, Finnish towns were still comparatively rural in their lifestyle, and a kind of economic self-sufficiency still prevailed in the wooden houses along the grid-planned streets. Vegetables, berries and fruits were grown in the gardens, and people still kept animals. Even in the centre of Helsinki, the yards of the town houses had their own wells, baking houses, sheds, barns, outhouses and saunas. In other words, the sauna was a familiar element of the environment.

A truly urban lifestyle did not set in until the 1880s, when so-called conveniences such as water mains, plumbing and electric lighting gradually became available and large masonry buildings began to replace the small wooden houses. Amidst this new technology, the sauna was no longer regarded as one of the conveniences of urban living.

The sauna was now set aside, particularly after the spread of the bathtub, which was introduced around the turn of the century and which became popular in the 1920s. People were so enthralled by this innovation that they had little need for the sauna for their daily or weekly bathing. The bathtub also carried connotations of European opulence, and in comparison, the sauna seemed old-fashioned and rural.

But the sauna did not completely disappear from the urban scene. It only retreated into the outskirts and suburbs of towns, where it discovered its natural place on small lots. This new environment saw the development of a completely new type of sauna in the yards of single-family houses.

The sauna was no longer a separate building; it was placed in an outbuilding serving other functions, usually next to a woodshed and the outhouse and other facilities necessary for the upkeep of the property. It no longer "looked like a sauna", being hidden behind the unassuming walls of the outbuildings. But in compensation for losing its image, it gained extra space: a separate dressing room, which often served as a spare bedroom for overnight guests or tenants.

The materials of the sauna also underwent a fundamental change when a framework of boarding replaced the traditional log construction. The walls were boarded on both sides of the upright framework, with insulation of sawdust and shavings. The floor was now a solid slab of concrete ground to a smooth finish. The sheet-metal upright stove was now accompanied by a large metal container for heating water and washing laundry.

But the insulation of the interior walls was generally less than perfect and a great deal of water was used in the sauna, often the only place to wash, rot fungus would spread rapidly in the structures that often remained wet for long periods. Since the wet concrete floor developed mildew as it dried slowly, the smell of rot and mildew was often the first impression of the sauna. Adding to this the fact that firewood was used sparingly and the stove gave little heat, and even that was mostly steam near the ceiling, it is no surprise that many Finnish children of the 1920 and '30s do not have very fond memories of their home saunas.

Public saunas

In the early decades of the twentieth century, the inhabitants of apartment buildings had to make do without their own saunas. But fortunately there were public saunas, run as business enterprises, in the towns and cities.

Public saunas had existed in Finland since the early nineteenth century. Some of these establishments advertised themselves as baths or spas. In addition to attendants who washed the customers, the best saunas had masseurs, blood-letters ("cuppers") and even chiropractors. There was an evident desire to follow the trends of baths and spas, which had been established in Finland in the eighteenth century. The standards of public saunas were maintained, even to the degree that in 1807 the medical authorities laid down that the attendants of public saunas should have some knowledge of German and Latin. In later years, however, most of the public saunas were modest establishments serving the common people. In these local saunas a knowledge of Finnish was more than sufficient for the attendants.

Well-equipped public saunas had separate departments for men and women, as well as dressing and washing rooms and smaller stove rooms that could be hired for family use. The public section was naturally open to all corners. The men's and women's saunas were served by a single stove. The stove lids were open on both sides and the male and female bathers could engage in light banter.

In the Rajaportti public sauna in Tampere, built in 1906, men and women first bathed together, although they had separate dressing rooms. There was nothing strange about this –

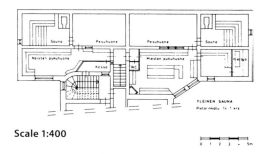

Scale 1:400

Fig. 13. Public sauna at 14 Pietarinkatu street, Helsinki. The men's and women's departments are on the first floor. Private saunas for hire are on the second floor. Measured drawing by Toni Parkkima.

nudism was still an unknown word. Some time later, a textile curtain was installed to separate the men from the women, and eventually a wall of masonry was built to divide the sauna and the washing room into two departments. As late as the 1920s there were mixed saunas at least at Tampere and Kristiinankaupunki.

The Rajaportti sauna still displays its special design. It is almost five metres high and split into two levels. Uppermost is the platform, originally of wood and now of concrete, beneath which are the washing areas. This made it possible to enjoy the heat and to cool off in the same space.

In the overall development of saunas, the public sauna is an offshoot of the Finnish sauna and specifically Finnish customs. It is closely related to the banya, the Russian public saunas which have operated in cities and towns for centuries.

The main difference between the old Finnish sauna and the public sauna is that the former is one's own and a private place, while the latter is open to all and used by all. The private sauna

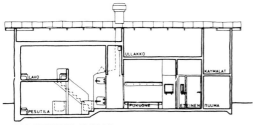
LONGITUDINAL SECTION

UPPER FLOOR

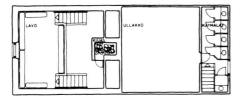
PLATFORM

Fig. 14. A public sauna in Tampere. There are separate dressing rooms for men and women, but the stove room and the washing area under the platforms are in common use. This sauna at Rajaportti was later divided in two with a partition.

walls and ceiling were plastered and painted.

The public saunas are humid "steam baths" like the Russian banya. A lot of water is thrown on the stones as bathers come and go, and there is a great deal of moisture in the air. It has been estimated that in the old smoke saunas only some four litres of water were used by each bather; in public saunas the corresponding figure is 150–200 litres. There was also the added humidity of condensed water remaining on cool masonry surfaces.

Public saunas remained popular until the 1940s. One reason was that rationing regulations restricted the amount of hot water a single household could use, while in the public saunas more of it was available. But in later years, one public sauna after another has had to close down, as the saunas of swimming baths began to compete for their customers, most of whom now started to move into new suburbs with saunas in the apartment buildings. There are now efforts to keep some of the remaining public saunas in operation as "museum saunas".

The electric sauna

Following the invention of stove with flues, the electrically heated stove was the next major development in the history of the sauna, marking the third generation of saunas.

It is said that where there's a will, there's a way. This is also true of the electric sauna. According to Pirkko Valtakari, writing in the journal Sauna, an office building, including a sauna, was constructed in 1938 in Vaasa. The building inspectors, however, noted that the flue was incorrectly installed and accordingly could not permit the use of the sauna. To find a quick remedy to the situation, it was decided to construct a

has only one, or at most two, rooms, while the public sauna has several rooms to serve different needs.

The materials are also different: one is of wood, while the other is of stone and masonry. The latter aspect gave public saunas a specific image and atmosphere which included the echoes of masonry walls. The floors were of concrete, sometimes painted or laid with tiles; the

Fig. 15. A sauna in a Helsinki apartment building from 1938. The only access from the dressing rooms to the washing room and the stove room is through a corridor. The flue of the wood-fired stove is on the outside wall. From *Talosauna* by Erkki Helamaa.

stove that required no flues at all. This is the claimed origin of the electrically heated sauna.

It was soon discovered that the lack of flues was a great advantage. Electric saunas could be built in places where it was either impossible or difficult to install the wood-fired stoves. This removed, again, a number of restrictions posed by the sauna stove. Only half a century previously had the stoves with flues replaced the old smoke stove and opened up new possibilities for the sauna.

The electric sauna stove is easy to use and maintain. The stones are heated by electric resistor elements and there is no need to arrange firewood. All that is needed is the flick of a switch, a timer setting, or activation by telephone.

Block saunas

In the late 1940s, the spread of electric sauna stoves was a factor promoting the construction of saunas in blocks of flats and apartments. These are used by the inhabitants according to set schedules. In most cases, the sauna is in the basement, though sometimes in the attic or in a separate building.

A number of saunas were already built in apartment houses in the 1930s, but these were not the same as their present-day counterparts. Such saunas were usually built in a cellar adjacent to the wood store of the building. Proper attention to this facility in apartment houses did not begin until 1949 when the state-managed Arava organization for urban development began its work.

One aspect of this development was a sauna guide written by L.M. Viherjuuri. The first version of this book in 1944 mentions nothing about saunas in apartment buildings, although there is much information on various kinds of saunas, and the author notes that public saunas are the only ones available to city dwellers. A later version in 1955 mentions the apartment-building saunas as a new type of sauna.

Wood-fired stoves were difficult to use and maintain in the apartment buildings, and leading the flues all the way from the basement to the roof required labour and materials. It also placed restrictions on the design of the actual sauna and the apartments above it. Heating the stove – every day in large buildings – also required a great deal of time and effort.

The electric stove, on the other hand, was a carefree solution, but for some reason government housing authorities were long suspicious

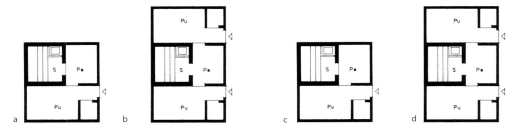

S = STOVE ROOM   Pe = WASHING ROOM   Pu = DRESSING ROOM

Fig. 16. Combinations of rooms and space in a block sauna: a) well functioning unit consisting of a dressing room, a washing room and stove room; b) a highly popular combination of two dressing rooms, one washroom and a stove room; c) an efficient system of two dressing rooms, two washing rooms and a stove room, which requires a stopwatch for bathing; d) a combination of four dressing rooms, two washing rooms and a stove room, with no peace and quiet for enjoying the bath. From *Talosauna* by Erkki Helamaa.

of it. It was not until 1968 that specific planning instructions to avoid electrically heated sauna stoves were revised.

The basic type of sauna in an apartment building is one with a dressing room, a shower room and the sauna itself. More effective variants permitting more frequent use are ones with two dressing rooms and two shower rooms respectively. There are even designs with as many four dressing rooms and two shower rooms. The only thing lacking is the peace and quiet of the sauna.

In the late 1970s there were signs of a decline in the construction of block saunas. They had found a competitor – the sauna in the apartment itself.

The apartment sauna

In the mid-1970s apartment buildings dominated housing construction in Finland. As changes towards smaller housing units were slow to implement, developers and builders tried to introduce into apartments the traditional features of single-family houses. Balconies were enlarged to compensate for outdoor space and more auxiliary rooms and facilities were built. In this connection, the sauna established itself in apartments as an appendage to the bathroom.

Although small apartment buildings were only a short-lived phenomenon, this type of housing was to have a profound influence on the sauna, by introducing this essentially Finnish feature into apartments.

In larger numbers and in their present configurations, saunas in apartments began to be built in the late 1960s and early '70s in the Olari suburb of Espoo, adjoining Helsinki. These examples were first followed quite reluctantly. Only a few construction firms operating in Espoo installed apartment saunas, and it was not until the mid-l970s that the concept began to spread, for the above-mentioned reasons, to become a feature with which apartments were sold. At present, a small sauna of this kind has almost become a standard feature of apartments.

The main problem of this type of sauna is space – to a compounded degree. It is first encountered in the apartment as a whole, where the miniature sauna requires part of what is already limited room. A further problem of space is in the sauna itself. The apartment saunas are very small, on the average only 2.3 square metres in floor area; the smallest ones measure 1.4 square metres.

A small sauna is more of a sweat-box than a proper sauna. To avoid the impression that this is only criticism for criticism's sake, a brief explanation is called for.

In the sauna the bather feels the heat partly via convection (through the medium of the air) and partly through radiation; the heat of the platform is not important. In addition to the stove, heat radiates from the walls and ceiling. In a good sauna, heat is conveyed symmetrically, which means that the bather feels heat evenly from all directions and there is a balance between convected and radiated heat. The bather should also be able to sit at a proper distance from the source of radiated heat. In a small apartment sauna, where the stove is almost in one's lap and all other radiating surfaces are very close, the situation is much like a grill. There is no symmetry of heat, and radiation largely predominates over convected heat. The steam and heat from the water thrown on the stones hits one in the eye, because there is no sufficiently large buffer of air between the stove and the bather.

The sauna by the shore

In the nineteenth century, romantic poets and writers praised the natural beauty of Finland with her forests and lake shores. The poet J.L. Runeberg wrote of the land of a thousand lakes. Runeberg, unfortunately, was wrong – surveyors and cartographers have counted as many as 187,000 lakes in Finland. All this has led us to believe that we have access to innumerable lake shores where we can build our saunas. At present, there are some 400,000 lakeside saunas, many of which are eyesores in otherwise idyllic surroundings.

The sauna by the shore is nevertheless a relatively late aspect of what sociologists have come to call the 'summer migration', with its roots going back to the ancient Romans. In the summer, the noble of families of Rome used to flee the heat of the city to the countryside. In Finland, such customs began in the mid-seventeenth century when professors at the Academy of Turku chose to spend their summers in the country, mainly farming their own or rented holdings. The late eighteenth century idealized nature and the rural life, and many of the urban upper classes moved for the summer from the towns to the countryside. This custom first began in the coastal towns of Ostrobothnia, and it soon spread to Finland Proper and other regions. By the middle of the nineteenth century, spending the summer at a villa became so common among upper-class families that complete villa communities were established. For example, in Turku the city authorities rented some fifty villa sites in nearby Ruissalo.

The summer villas were impressive and comfortable houses where guests could be received. They were also intended to demonstrate the wealth and standing of their owners. But they had no saunas, nor were such desired, for the villa owners were mostly Swedish-Finns, who were not accustomed to the sauna, and even the Finnish-speaking upper-class families regarded the sauna as a custom of the common people.

After the first world war a number of pro-

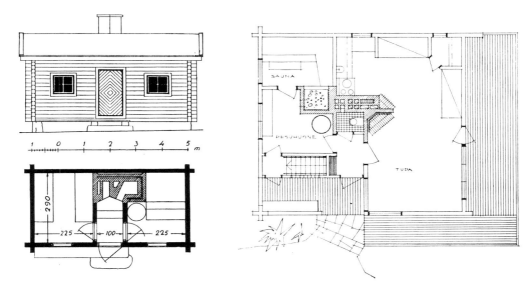

Fig. 17. The "Tuusula sauna" designed in the 1930s by H.J. Viherjuuri and Veikko Leisten was meant to be a standard type of sauna for shore locations. From *Saunaopas* by H.J. Viherjuuri.

Fig. 18. A lakeshore sauna cottage. Architects A. Hytönen and R.-V. Luukkonen, early 1950's. Scale 1:150. From *The Finnish Architectural Review Arkkitehti* 3–4/1952.

found changes came about in Finnish society and among the Finns themselves, in a country that had recently gained its independence. These changes were seen and felt in all quarters. Working-class people now began to enjoy benefits such as paid summer vacations, and dwellings for leisure use soon became available to all. A mass movement in this area did not begin until the 1950s, when the general standard of living began to rise after war reparations and reconstruction. The summer dwellings underwent a number of changes in their ownership and use. The impressive villa was now replaced by a summer cottage, which included a sauna.

The sauna often has the leading role in the life Finns lead at their summer cottages. It is heated almost every day, and many cottages have evolved around a sauna that was built first. An ensemble with a stove room, washing room, veranda, living room, cooking and sleeping areas, all under one roof, contains all the elements of a Finnish leisure home and sauna.

In the long history of the sauna, these leisure saunas signify a return to nature and the original roots of the sauna. Although there are exceptions, such as barrel-shaped saunas and overly romantic log structures, these leisure saunas evidence a return to simple forms and natural materials.

2. The Planning and Design of a Sauna

This chapter is on the design of the rooms and space required in a sauna and their various functions. It also discusses the location of a sauna in the terrain and inside other buildings, and gives instructions on the dimensioning of saunas.

General Remarks

The layout and dimensioning of the rooms and space required in a sauna, the furnishings of the sauna and the design of its details are influenced by the following factors:
– users
– method of use
– location
– method of heating (stove type)

Users
A sauna may have a single user (or group of users), or its users may vary continuously.

Method of use
Depending on use, the sauna can be heated at repeated, though not intermittent, intervals, e.g. once a week, or it may be in use almost continuously, being heated for long periods at a time.

Location
The sauna can be either a separate building or in connection with other rooms, such as service facilities, workspaces, recreation rooms or maintenance rooms in buildings. In the following, saunas are divided into separate sauna buildings and those in connection with other rooms and facilities.

Method of heating (stove type)
The sauna stove is usually heated with firewood or electricity. It can also be heated with oil, bottled or natural gas.

The choice of heating method affects the construction and functioning of the stove, as also the dimensions of the sauna itself.

Concepts

The term sauna can mean any of the following:
- a room where bathers seated on platforms perspire in the heat of the stove, throw water on the stove stones, and wash themselves.
- a building or group of rooms with the above sauna and other rooms. All the different stages of the sauna bath are conducted here: perspiring, washing, cooling, resting and dressing.
- a heated sauna and the bathing carried out there.

The stove room (Fi. löylyhuone) is a technical term meaning the actual sauna room with the stove as opposed to other parts of the sauna.

A sauna department or unit consists of one or several saunas and their auxiliary rooms and is connected with rooms and space for other functions, such as a swimming baths, a gymnasium, or a care establishment, or it can be a separate series of rooms, such as a sauna in an apartment building.

The shore or summer sauna is of light construction and mainly intended for use in the warm months of the year.

Saunas grouped according to location and use

Separate saunas

The saunas of holiday or summer homes are in connection with a residence for leisure use and are located either in a separate building or as part of a holiday home.

The yard sauna is either a separate sauna building on the lot of a single-family or small house or forming part of an outbuilding.

Saunas in connection with other rooms and facilities

A block sauna is used jointly by several households in a row house or block of flats. It can be located in a basement or attic, in connection with the stairwell, or in a separate building in the courtyard.

A home sauna is a sauna belonging to a dwelling and used by a single household. It is, however, not directly connected to the dwelling or apartment but is located, for example, in a cellar or a separate wing.

An apartment sauna is a sauna directly connected to an apartment (usually in an apartment block or row house) and used by a single household.

A public sauna serves varying customers or groups and is usually in connection with a swimming baths, baths establishment or hotel. This category includes the former public saunas which were run as business enterprises.

Sauna stoves grouped according to heating methods

Stoves without flues

The smoke stove is made of unworked stones or bricks and is not connected to a flue. See Fig. 19.

Stoves with flues

The heat-storage stove is heated in a single process before bathing to a suitable temperature, whereby the heat is stored in the stones. See Fig. 19.

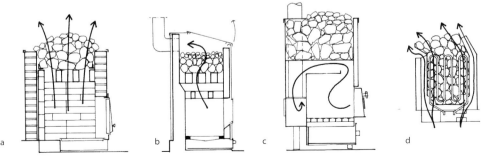

Fig. 19. Stove types. From the left a) flueless stove (smoke stove), b) heat-storage stove with flue, c) continuous heating stove with flue, and d) electric stove. Scale ca. 1:25

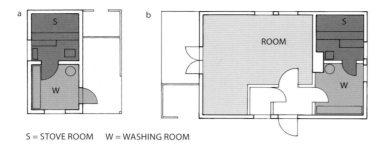 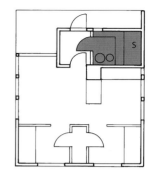

S = STOVE ROOM   W = WASHING ROOM

Fig. 20. Saunas for holiday homes. a) Lakeside sauna (summer sauna). b) Sauna for year-round use. Scale 1:200.

Fig. 21. Sauna for a holiday cabin. Scale 1:200.

The continuous heating stove can be heated during the bathing, as the firewood burns in a separate chamber and the flames do not pass through the stones, Fig. 19.

Electric stoves

In the electric stove heat produced electrically is led from resistors to the stove stones. See Fig. 19.

Stoves heated with other fuels

Sauna stoves can also be heated with bottled and natural gas or oil.

The stoves are discussed in more detail in Chapters 5 and 7.

The Location of the Sauna and Related Functions

Summer and leisure saunas

The sauna is an essential feature of Finnish holiday homes. It can be a separate building, but if it includes other rooms it can be an interior facility similar to the apartment or home sauna.

The sauna building is generally sited close to a body of water. In order to preserve the natural landscape, the shoreline must remain untouched. To ensure this, various regulations have been passed concerning the minimum distance of buildings from the shoreline. These regulations vary according to locality.

In view of the needs of the landscape it is necessary to try to place the sauna building in the shelter of the terrain and trees growing at the site. Earth-moving works and quarrying that will permanently change the nature of the site must be avoided. The connection of the sauna building with its natural surroundings can be aided with the correct choice of building form, materials and colour.

A shore sauna (summer sauna), mainly used in the warm months of the year, can be simpler in its layout of space and lighter in construction than a sauna for regular year-round use. Fig. 20.

- The stove room is usually designed for four bathers. If it is also used for washing, a space

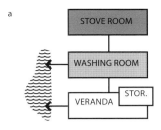
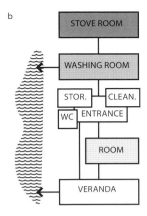

Fig. 22. Connections between various parts of a sauna at a holiday home. a) Summer sauna, b) Year-round sauna for a holiday home.

in front of the door is reserved for this purpose and for heating water.
- The washing room can be designed for two bathers, as a holiday sauna is usually in unhurried use. Space is also reserved for hot and cold water cisterns. The water is heated in a metal container connected to the stove, in a cistern located in the washing room with a heating pipe passing through the stove, an electrically heated container, or a separate cistern with its own fireplace.
- The dressing room is designed according to intended use. The bathers can also dress on a porch or veranda fitted with benches. The dressing room can also be a spacious and well-equipped dwelling room with cooking facilities and beds.
- The cooling area can be arranged in various ways. A simple solution is a bench by the wall or a porch in front of the entrance. It can also be a terrace with a grill and outdoor furniture.
- Important considerations are evening sunlight, privacy, protection from the wind, and a good view.
- The outhouse can be in joint use with the holiday home if the distance is not too great. If there is no sewer, a compost-type, chemical or electrically operated privy is used.
- Firewood can be stored in connection with the sauna, inside or in a separate shed.

The sauna in a building in the yard

In areas subject to zoning and planning regulations, the sauna in the yard area, i.e. for a single-family house or farmhouse, is located according to local regulations. Elsewhere, the siting principles of saunas for holiday homes are followed.

The sauna can also be in an outbuilding containing storage space, working areas and a garage.
- The sauna is usually dimensioned for four persons.
- The washing room is dimensioned for use by two persons simultaneously.

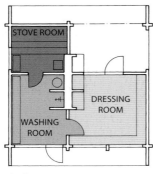

Scale 1:200.

Fig. 23. A sauna in the yard of a single-family house.

- The dressing room is dimensioned for four persons, and should have access via an entrance space. Farm saunas are fitted with a separate ventilated storage area for work clothes (size 3 m²).

A WC and storage space for cleaning equipment and firewood are also recommended.

A second sauna is often built inside the dwelling on a farmstead immediately adjacent to the bathroom, as an apartment-sauna type facility.

The block sauna

The block sauna is used by the inhabitants of an apartment building or row house according to a rota system. According to the Finnish custom, the sauna is usually owned and maintained by the building as a company of apartment owners.

A block sauna can be located in the basement, the attic, in connection with the stairwell, or in a separate service building.

- The stove room is usually dimensioned for four bathers. The door is to be wide enough to permit use by disabled persons. There must also be sufficient free space in front of the door.

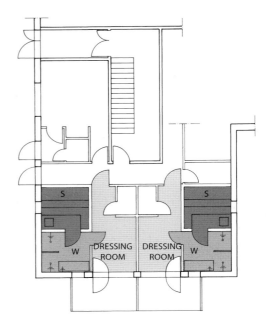

Fig. 24. Block sauna with two units. Scale 1:200.

- The washing room is to have at least two showers and a hose connection to provide water for throwing on the stove. The washing room should also have a bench or a sufficient number of stools.
- The dressing room is dimensioned for four persons, and it should have a sufficient number of seats, a table, pegs, a mirror and a rubbish bin.

A further advantage is to have access from the building's possible meeting and recreation rooms to the sauna dressing room. See Fig. 24.

- The cooling area can be a terrace or balcony.
- The block sauna also requires a WC, a cleaning materials cupboard and storage space.

Fig. 25. Washing room in a block sauna.
Photo: Mina Jokivirta.

Fig. 26. Interior of sauna shown in Fig. 23. Sauna at the Hautala farm in Nivala. Designed by the architect Ilkka Pajamies.

Fig. 27. Dressing room in a block sauna.
Photo: Mina Jokivirta.

Fig. 28. Stove room in a block sauna.
The Finnish Sauna Society.

The home sauna

The home sauna, usually in a single-family or row house, is within the building and accessed from the other rooms and space, but situated apart from the actual apartment.

This type of sauna may be located in the basement, or in a house on a sloping site on the side against the slope, or in a service wing on the same level as the apartment.

The planning of a sauna in a basement or cellar may come across problems caused by the locations of bearing structures and various installations led downwards from the living area.

It is usually impossible to install windows in basement saunas on sloping sites.

A sauna in a separate service building or wing can be planned and designed as required with relatively few restrictions.

- The stove room is usually dimensioned for four bathers, and it should function together with the other rooms.
- The washing room is dimensioned for the use of two persons at the same time. The room has two showers, one of which has a hose outlet to provide water for the stove room. Alternatively, there can be a separate tap near the door to the stove room.
- The dressing room is designed for use by 4–6 persons.
- In connection with the home sauna, a separate WC and a possible cooling and lounging room with a fireplace can be planned.

Fig. 29. A large home sauna. Photo: SunSauna.

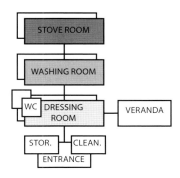

Fig. 30. Connections between the parts of a block sauna.

Fig. 31. Connections between the various parts of a home sauna.

Fig. 32. Floor plan of a home sauna.

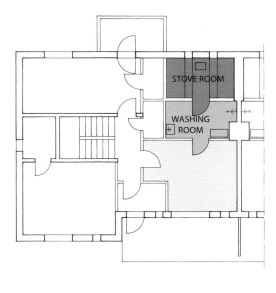

Fig. 33. Sauna in the basement of a semi-detached house on a sloping site. Scale 1:200.

Fig. 34. Washing room in an apartment sauna.

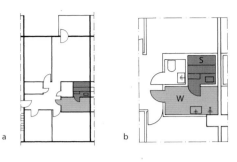

S = STOVE ROOM   W = WASHING ROOM

Fig. 35. Saunas located within a building: a) scale 1:500; b) scale 1:200.

The apartment sauna

The apartment sauna is a sauna directly connected to the apartment (in a block of flats or row house and sometimes in a single-family house).

It is suggested that this sauna is located adjacent to the exterior, whereby at least one of its sides is an exterior wall. This will permit the installation of a window and an air intake vent. The sauna can also be placed in the middle of the building, in which case it will have no window and the incoming air must be led from outside.

In planning a sauna for an apartment, access to the dressing location and the balcony should be taken into consideration.
- The sauna (stove room) is dimensioned for two bathers.
  In apartments of two rooms and a kitchen (or larger ones) in row and semi-detached houses either the washing room or the stove room is to have a window. This is also recommended for apartment saunas in blocks of flats.
- The washing room is to be planned with at least one shower. If there are two showers, one of them is to have a tap for providing water for the stove room, or there should be a separate tap near the door to the stove room.
- The apartment sauna should have a separate WC, and it is also recommended that the washing machine and the household's dirty laundry be kept elsewhere than in the washing room.
- If there is no separate room for household work, appliances that generate humidity, such as washing machines and dryers, can be

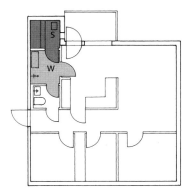

Fig. 36. Apartment sauna. Scale 1:200.

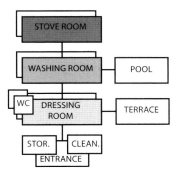

Fig. 37. Connections between the various parts of a public sauna.

placed in the washing room, but in such a location that they do not interfere with the bathing. These appliances require separate space.
- In most cases it is not possible to arrange a separate dressing room in a small apartment, but there should be a natural access from the washing room to an area suitable for this purpose.
- The apartment balcony is a suitable cooling area, if it is easily accessed.

Public saunas

These are saunas serving various bathers or groups, and used publicly by paying customers.

The old public saunas in Finnish towns and cities offered local inhabitants the only possibility to bathe in a sauna, but at present they have almost completely disappeared.

Present-day public saunas are the sauna facilities of swimming baths, gymnasiums, baths establishments, rehabilitation centres and hotels.

- Public saunas have separate departments for men and women. They also provide separate saunas that can be hired by groups of people.
- The number of bathers in public saunas varies according to the groups concerned and the time of day. The necessary rooms and facilities are to be planned and dimensioned according to the number of visitors in the peak hours of an average day.
- Also to be considered are requirements of comfort, which usually mean the construction of stove rooms of different size. The largest sauna (several units where necessary) is dimensioned for 12–16 persons and the smaller ones for 4–6 persons.
- The washing rooms should have at least five showers each. Also required is a tap with a hose plug for cleaning purposes.

THE PLANNING AND DESIGN OF A SAUNA

Planning of Rooms and Space in Saunas

Instructions for dimensioning according to numbers of bathers are given in the section on The location of the sauna and related functions.

The stove room

The size and dimensioning of the sauna (stove room) depends upon:
– the number of bathers
– the locations of the platforms
– the space required by the stove
– the method of heating

Dimensioning

Room height in a stove room is usually 2000–2200 mm. With present room heights the space between the platform level and the ceiling is 1000–1200 mm.

The height of the stove room is traditionally defined according to the level of the stones on the stove, with the intention that feet of the seated bather are above the stones. At present, it is maintained that the whole space should be suitably hot for bathing.

In large facilities, such as public saunas, higher rooms are required to provide sufficient air.

The stove

The various types of stoves according to the method of heating are presented in the section Concepts and in Fig. 19.

A flueless smoke stove constructed in the stove room requires the greatest amount of space. The construction of smoke stoves is discussed in Chapter 7. Wood-fired factory-made stoves require somewhat more space than electric stoves. The additional space required by the

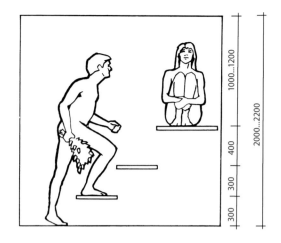

Fig. 38. Height requirements in a sauna.

various stoves is taken into account in the illustrations of platform locations. The stoves are fitted with a protective barrier.

Further information on stoves and safety considerations concerning distances from them is given in Chapter 5. The necessary electric installations are presented in Chapter 6.

The platforms

Minimum platform length recommended in saunas is 1800 mm. Recommended platform length per person is 600 mm.

Exceptionally the platform may be 1500 mm long. The width of the sitting platform is 400–900 mm and that of the platform for the feet and the step is 300–400 mm. The step should not be more than 300 mm high.

The platforms are either straight and aligned along one wall, or are in L- or U-shaped ar-

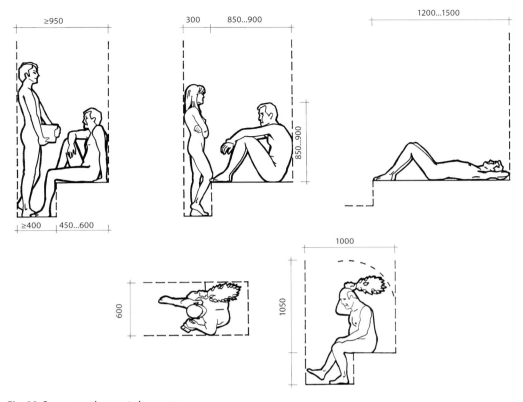

Fig. 39. Space requirements in a sauna.

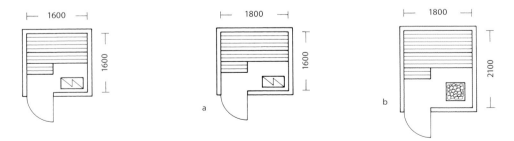

Fig. 40. An electrically heated sauna for two persons. Only in small apartments. Scale 1:100.

Fig. 41. Three-person saunas: a) electric stove, b) stove with a flue. Scale 1:100.

THE PLANNING AND DESIGN OF A SAUNA

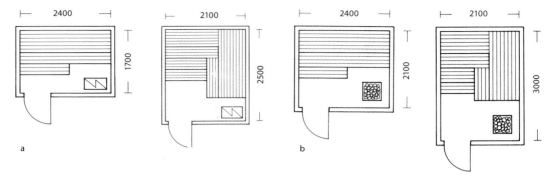

Fig. 42. Four-person saunas: a) electric stove, b) stove with a flue. Scale 1:100.

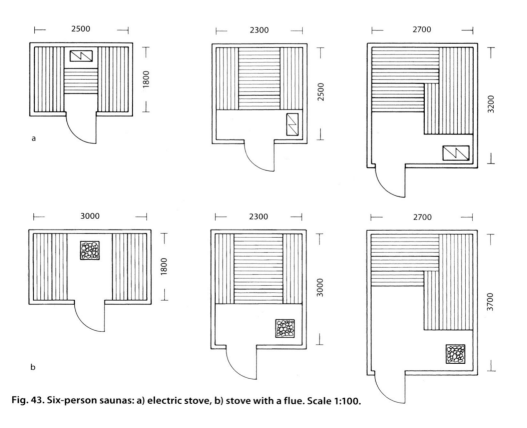

Fig. 43. Six-person saunas: a) electric stove, b) stove with a flue. Scale 1:100.

Fig. 44. Platforms in an L-shaped configuration. The Finnish Building Industry Confederation. Photo: Teemu Töyrylä.

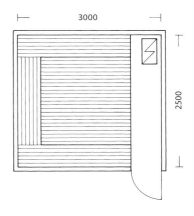

Fig. 45. Electrically heated sauna for 14 persons. Scale 1:100.

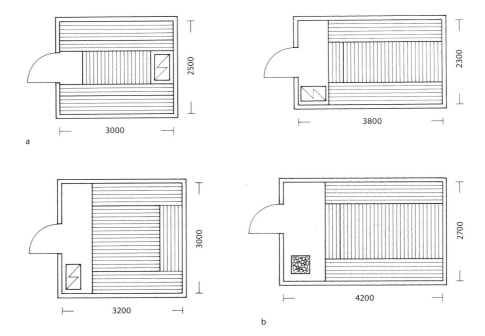

Fig. 46. Saunas for ten persons: a) electric stove b) stove with a flue. Scale 1:100.

THE PLANNING AND DESIGN OF A SAUNA | 41

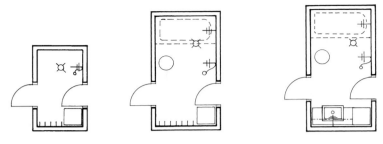

Fig. 47. Washing rooms for home and apartment saunas. Scale 1:100.

Fig. 48. Sauna with facing platforms and an electric stove. Photo: Kastor Oy.

rangements. The straight platform is the most usual type and the simplest in construction. The dimensioning and constructions of the platforms are given in Chapter 4.

Fenestration

There should be windows in the dressing, washing and bathing rooms of a sauna.

In apartments of two rooms and a kitchen (or larger ones) in row and semi-detached houses either the washing room or the stove room should have a window.

If the sauna has no windows, there should be a glass surface in the door between the stove room and the washing room.

In addition to providing light, the sauna window is also intended to create the mood of the sauna, to make the small room appear larger, and to facilitate ventilation after the bath. The sauna window can be very small. The traditional manner is to place the window at a low elevation, whereby most of the light falls on the floor in front of the stove. It is not recommended to place the window behind the platforms, as the bathers would then have to sit with their backs to it.

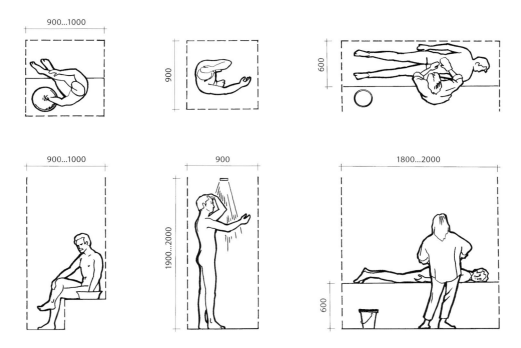

Fig. 49. Space requirements for washing. Scale 1:50.

The door

Access from the door to the platforms should be protected and at a sufficient distance from the hot stove. If the stove is next to the door, it should be hinged on the stove side. The door to a wood-heated sauna should be near the door.

The door should have no threshold, and should open outwards from the stove room. There should be a gap of at least 50 mm beneath it, and the door should be fitted with a roller catch. The pull should be of wood. Requirements for disabled persons are presented in the section Planning a sauna for use by disabled persons.

The washing room

The size and dimensioning of the washing room depend on the number of persons washing at the same time and on the necessary fixtures and furnishings. Space required for washing is shown in Fig. 49.

The showers should be spaced at least 900 mm apart (not including partitions).

Equipment and furnishings

The furniture of the washing room consists of stools and benches. In block and public saunas benches alone are used in the washing rooms. These may be movable or fixed in place.

Also required in the washing room are mois-

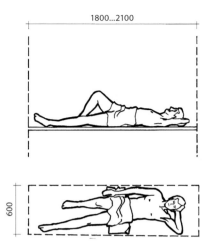

Fig. 50. Space required for dressing.

ture-resistant shelves and cupboards for washing gear. Pegs and drying racks are needed for towels.

Sound insulation in washing rooms is discussed in Chapter 3, and the furnishings are presented in Chapter 4.

The dressing room

The dimensioning of the dressing room depends on how the sauna is used, the number of bathers, and the fixtures required for dressing.

The furnishings of the dressing room are discussed in Chapter 4.

Other rooms

Lounging area

In holiday homes and apartments the living room, a room with a fireplace, or a room in connection with the sauna serves as a lounging area. A similar room is also recommended for block saunas, for example a room with a fireplace or a meeting room in connection with several sauna units. A sufficiently large lounging area is necessary in public saunas.

Cooling area

An essential part of enjoying the sauna is to be able to cool off in fresh air, on a veranda, balcony or terrace. This area should be shielded from view and wind, and if possible should face the setting sun and a scenic view.

The swimming pool

The swimming pool is located near the washing room. Instead of a swimming pool there can be a Jacuzzi pool used for refreshing oneself, water massage, or bathing. The purification equipment should meet sufficient efficiency requirements.

Cleaning facilities

Block and public saunas are special area of buildings requiring space for a cleaning cupboard or a room with a sink and tap, and storage space for equipment.

Storage facilities

Depending on the use of the sauna, storage space is required for the following:
– firewood
– birch whisks
– clean and used towels and bathrobes
– seat covers
– washing gear
– refreshments

If there is no separate cleaning cupboard or room, space must be set apart for this purpose.

Planning a Sauna for Use by Disabled Persons

Public buildings and areas must be designed to suit the disabled without resorting to special arrangements. They would accordingly be better suited to the needs of children and the elderly, and all sectors of the public. Private saunas can be planned and designed according to specific handicaps or with provisions for the presence of an assistant.

The stove room

Persons using wheelchairs use a special shower chair in the sauna. This requires a minimum of 1500 x 1500 mm of unrestricted floor area to permit turning. The floor should not be slippery when wet, and the stove should be protected to prevent the person from burning himself. The feet of a person in a shower chair are in particular danger, and it is therefore necessary to extend the protective construction lower than would normally be the case.

The free width of the doorway should be a minimum of 800 mm.

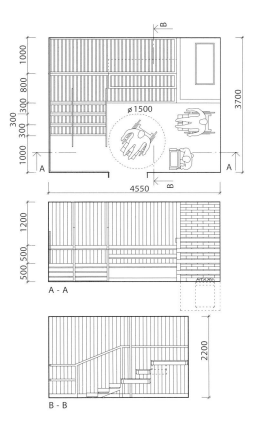

Fig. 51. Sauna for disabled persons.

With normal platform and stove elevations, disabled persons require a sauna of larger floor area than normally. If the stove is designed as to provide steam and heat to the lowermost platforms, there will be no need for high platforms. This solution permits, within the same area, either a normal design with platforms or a platformless sauna with only benches.

The difficulty of climbing onto the platforms can also be eradicated on a sloping site by placing the stove room lower than the washing room. Accordingly the door would open onto the lower platform level, permitting access from the shower chair directly to the platform at the corresponding level.

Various railings can be used to assist access to the platforms. A person using a shower chair will find it easier to move to the lowest platform if it is at the same height as the chair, i.e. ca. 500 mm from floor level. Moving from one platform to another by hand is possible if the maximum difference in height is 300 mm.

The washing room

The floor of the washing room should be inclined only to the degree necessary for gathering the water. Covering the floor is not recommended. Special attention is to be paid to the non-slip characteristics and ease of cleaning of the floor surface. A depression of the floor under the showers is not recommended.

Hand grips are to be installed in the walls, particularly in connection with the showers at 500 and 900 mm above floor level. Round tubing is recommended (diameter 30–40 mm, 45 mm from the wall). It is also a good idea to install hand grips on other walls to facilitate access to the sauna.

The dressing room

Hand grips are placed at 500 mm and 900 mm above floor level on the dressing-room walls. Thresholds should be avoided in the design. If necessary, a flexible rubber threshold can be installed. In addition to a normal pull on the door leading from the dressing room to the washing room, a round-section metal pull is to be installed on the hinge side at a height of 800 mm to permit closing the door.

The dressing room will include a bench permitting the disabled person to dress in a lying position. The minimum dimensions of the bench are: length 2000 mm, height 500 mm and width 600–700 mm. A grid or duckboard covering the floor is not recommended. The floor should have an easily cleaned surface that will not be slippery when wet.

3. Planning the Components and Elements of a Sauna

This chapter discusses the various constructions and elements of the sauna. Instructions and examples are given concerning walls, floors, ceilings, intermediary floors and roofing according to specific building types and the choice of materials and their treatment in the stove room, washing room and dressing room.

General Remarks

In the stove room and the washing room vapour pressure, considerable differences of exterior and interior temperature and the intermittent use of the sauna place requirements on components and elements differing from those in other types of buildings.

The platforms are discussed in Chapter 4, and the stoves in Chapter 5.

Thermal Insulation

The heat-storage properties of the walls and roof can be influenced through the choice of structures and building elements.

If the walls and ceiling of the stove room are of masonry, the interior surfaces are fitted with an additional insulating layer, usually of mineral wool.

The floor of a sauna in continuous use is thermally insulated. The insulation of the floor corresponds to that of other adjoining moist rooms. Here, mineral wool or cellular plastic is used.

The thermally insulated floors of the sauna and the washing room can be equipped with water-circulation or electric heating elements, installed during casting in the topping layer. A floor of this kind is pleasant to walk on and dries rapidly.

The floors of holiday or summer saunas can be built of wood and left uninsulated. Mineral wool is a suitable insulating material for the walls. Sawdust and other loose insulation will in time descend to the lower parts, vacating the upper section, where the greatest amount of insulation is required.

Thermal insulation is discussed in more detail under the heading Components and elements.

Fig. 52. The platform supports left within the wall are affixed at the same level on both sides of the vapour barrier. Photo: Rauno Träskelin.

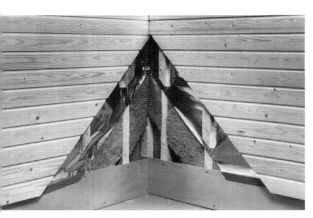

Fig. 53. Sauna wall. From the left: framework and mineral wool layer vapour barrier, battening for ventilation gap, interior boarding. Photo: Rauno Träskelin.

Water and Moisture Insulation

The components and elements surrounding the sauna are to be insulated against water and moisture to prevent damage to them or adjacent wall surfaces.

Owing to the high temperatures and humidity of the sauna, special attention must be paid to the transmission of vapour within components and elements. If the vapour in the air is freely admitted into the components, it can condense in the thermal insulation layer, thus weakening its effectivity and ultimately damaging it.

The components of a sauna unit in a building must be properly insulated to prevent moisture from spreading into other rooms and areas. Well-insulated components require efficient ventilation to dry the sauna after use.

The components are fitted with a vapour barrier made of heat-resistant vapour-proof plastic or paper faced with reflective aluminium foil. In the latter case, the reflecting surface is placed facing the interior (the sauna). The vapour barrier is installed in the walls and roof on the warm side of the thermal insulation.

The vapour insulation should have as few seams as possible and perforations should be avoided. All parts where elements pass through the insulation must be insulated with care. The overlaps must be at least 150 mm wide, affixed with heat-resistant tape, and pressed against each other between two wood surfaces. If the overlap coincides with the framework, the vapour barrier can be affixed with a batten. The corners, the points where the roof and walls meet, and the parts around openings are insulated with additional strips 200 mm wide.

Where a masonry wall joins a wooden roof-space floor or ceiling, the vapour barrier must form an airtight join with the inner surface of the thermal insulation.

The joins of door and window frames and the walls can be insulated with insulating foam or insulating tape to prevent moisture from entering. A vapour barrier placed between the framework and the interior boarding does not ensure sufficient insulation.

In an exterior wall built on a wooden framework an exterior wind barrier is required. This is made of specially fabricated boarding or building paper. The structures must be planned to permit the evaporation of moisture gathered in them. The wind barrier must permit the passage of vapour.

The floors of damp sauna rooms on the upper floors of dwellings are to be insulated with a bitumen mat or a water-proof floor covering. Plastic mats with welded seams are suitable floor coverings for moist rooms.

Components and Building Elements

Walls

The walls of the sauna can be of logs, beams or masonry. In a sauna located in connection with other rooms, insulating materials and surface finishing required by the use of the sauna are added to the components. In a separate sauna building, the exterior walls are usually of logs or beams.

Log is a suitable material for the exterior of a sauna not only as a traditional feature but also because of its technical properties. A log wall will store heat throughout and its temperature changes slowly. A log sauna will require a great deal of thermal energy to heat properly and consequently this material is suited to saunas with stoves that heat slowly. The walls absorb moisture from the water thrown on the stones and from the open air, which will preserve the scent of the timber for a long time.

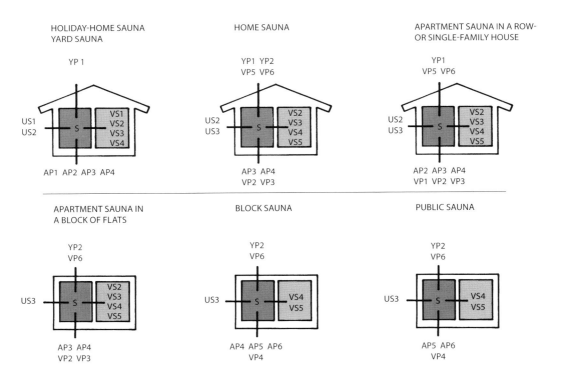

Fig. 54. Combinations of structures and components. The components to a scale of 1:20 and their connections are presented on following pages.

PLANNING THE COMPONENTS AND ELEMENTS OF A SAUNA

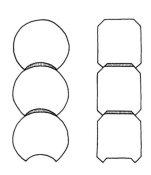 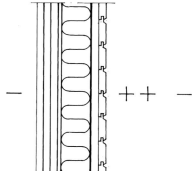 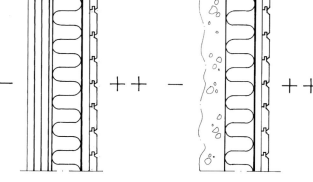

US 1 (VS 1)
- log wall
- ventilation gap and water-proof protective board at the location of the shower in the washing room

US 2
- external wall with thermal insulation as designed
- air and vapour barrier, e.g. aluminium-foil paper (not necessary in summer sauna)
- ventilation gap ≥20mm with corresponding battening
- interior finish

US 3 (VS 5)
- external masonry wall with thermal insulation as designed
- framework and thermal insulation (mineral wool)
- air and vapour barrier, e.g. aluminium-foil paper
- ventilation gap ≥20mm with corresponding battening
- interior finish

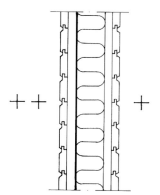 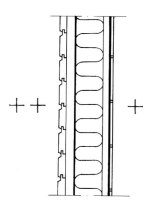 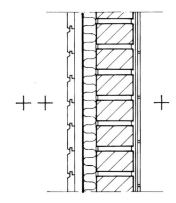

VS 2
- interior finish of stove room
- ventilation gap ≥20 mm and corresponding battening
- air and vapour barrier, e.g. aluminium-foil paper
- framework and thermal insulation (mineral wool 50–100 mm)
- ventilation gap ≥20 mm and corresponding battening
- interior finish of washing room
- ventilation gap and water-proof protective board at the location of the shower

VS 3
- interior finish of stove room
- ventilation gap ≥ 20 mm and corresponding battening
- air and vapour barrier, e.g. aluminium-foil paper
- framework and thermal insulation (mineral wool 50–100 mm)
- wallboard suitable for affixing tiles
- water-proofing according to manufacturer's instructions
- waterproof mortar or glue
- ceramic tiles

VS 4
- interior finish of stove room
- ventilation gap ≥ 20 mm and corresponding battening
- air and vapour barrier, e.g. aluminium-foil paper
- supporting members, thermal insulation (mineral wool 50–100 mm)
- brickwork
- facing mortar
- water-proof mortar
- ceramic tiles

Floors and ceilings

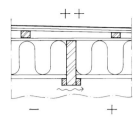

AP 2 (VP 1 with modifications)
- plastic mat with welded seams, affixed by glueing according to maker's instructions
- building board, specifications and installation according to manufacturer's instructions
- gradient with wedges ≥ 1:80
- building board
- lower or intermediary floor beams with thermal insulation as designed

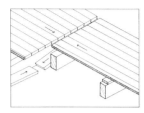

AP 1
- floor boards, maximum gap of ≥ 30 mm between the boards at the location of the water trough
- battening, gradient ≥ 1:30 towards trough, which may be of wood, plastic or metal. The water is led outside the building.
- beams

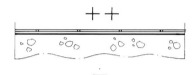

AP4
- ceramic tiles
- water-proof mortar
- bonding layer
- water-proofing
- reinforced concrete slab against ground. Thermal insulation as designed. Gradient ≥ 1:80.

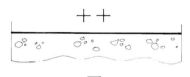

AP 3
- plastic mat with welded seams, affixed by glueing according to maker's instructions
- reinforced concrete slab against ground. Thermal insulation according to design. Gradient ≥ 1:80.

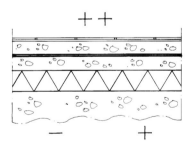

AP 6 (VP 4 with modifications)
- ceramic tiles
- water-proof mortar
- topping layer 50 mm, gradient finished when casting, heating elements installed if necessary
- anti-friction layer, plastic 0.2 mm + 0.2 mm
- water-proofing layer, bitumen mat, grade according to intended use
- reinforced concrete slab ≥ 50mm; gradient 1:50 minimum.
- thermal insulation of cellular polystyrene, thickness as according to structural design
- reinforced concrete or cavity block as according to structural design.

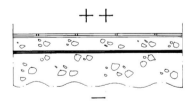

AP 5
- ceramic tiles
- waterproof mortar
- 50 mm topping layer; floor gradient finished in connection with casting, floor heating elements installed if necessary.
- anti-friction layer, plastic 0.2 mm + 0.2 mm
- water barrier, bitumen mat insulation, grade according to intended use of sauna
- reinforced concrete slab against ground. Thermal insulation as designed. Inclined ≥ 1:80

PLANNING THE COMPONENTS AND ELEMENTS OF A SAUNA

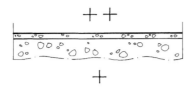 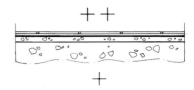

VP2
- plastic mat with welded seams, glued in place according to manufacturer's instructions.
- inclined concrete layer, gradient ≥ 1:80.
- reinforced concrete or cavity block as according to structural design

VP 3
- ceramic tiles
- waterproof mortar
- bonding layer
- water-proofing
- inclined concrete layer; gradient ≥ 1:80
- reinforced concrete or cavity block ceiling or intermediary floor as according to structural design

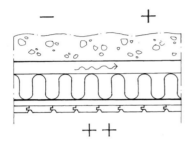 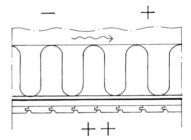

YP 1 (VP 5)
- ceiling or roof beam structure with thermal insulation as according to structural design.
- building board where required
- vapour barrier, e.g. aluminium-treated paper.
- ventilation gap ≥ 20mm and corresponding battening.
- interior lining of sauna

YP2(VP6)
- roof-space or ceiling structure of masonry with
- thermal insulation as according to structural design
- space ventilated from outside the sauna
- beam structure and thermal insulation, mineral wool 100 mm
- building board where necessary
- ventilation gap ≥ 20 mm and corresponding battening
- interior lining of sauna

Uninsulated smooth planed logs and similar components are mainly suited to saunas used only during the warm months of the year.

Prefabricated saunas are often made of thin board-like components, which cannot be regarded as log components as such.

The Roof

Choice of roofing material depends on the shape of the roof, its pitch, the desired appearance, and colour. Examples of roofing materials are bituminized felt, bituminized shingles, galvanized or plastic-coated sheet metal, ceramic or concrete roof tiles and fibre cement board.

The sauna can also be roofed with turf. The roof construction consists of felt roofing material overlaid by a drainage layer and two layers of turf. The eaves must be well ventilated. The weight of this roof construction must be taken into account in the dimensioning of the roof supports.

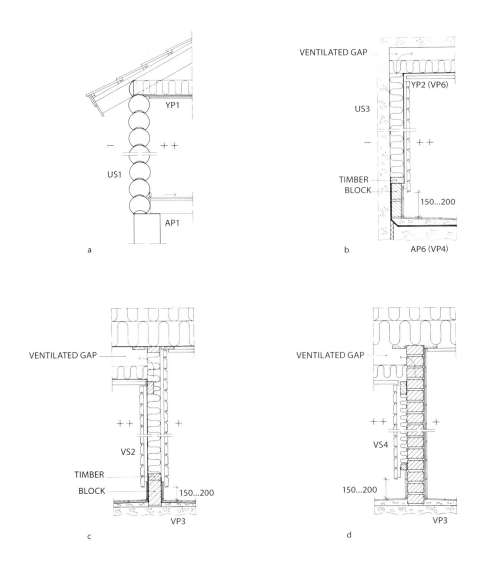

Fig. 55. a) Section of exterior sauna wall in a log building (summer sauna), b) section of exterior sauna wall in a masonry building c) wooden framework wall separating the sauna from the washing room, and d) masonry wall between the sauna and the washing room. In connection with the tiles there is a bituminized band. and an elastic seam at the point where the floor joins the wall. The vapour barrier of the wall is affixed to the lower surface of the joint of the frame, and the gap between the vapour barrier and the tiles is sealed with elastic putty. The space above the ceiling is ventilated from the adjacent dry rooms.

PLANNING THE COMPONENTS AND ELEMENTS OF A SAUNA

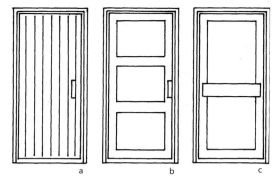

Fig. 56. Door types for saunas: a) panelled door b) door with glass panes or panels, c) glass door.

The doors

Door types suited to moist conditions are to be selected for the sauna. Examples of these are panelled doors and models with panels and glazing. See Fig. 56. The panelled door leading from the washing room to the stove room is faced with boarding on both sides and insulated against moisture. In most cases, the door is not fitted with thermal insulation. The sauna door can also be glazed to admit light and give a feeling of spaciousness. Vertical panelling is recommended. Two or three of the panels in a panel door can be replaced with panes of glass. In a triple glazed door of this type the bottom pane is usually of strengthened security glass. A door completely of glass is always made of strengthened security glass.

Additional Components

Windows and vents

The sauna windows are of similar construction as in other corresponding buildings. A twinglazed window that can be opened is usually sufficient for sauna at a holiday or summer home. The inner frame should be insulated to prevent vapour from condensing between the panes. In other sauna types, the windows are usually triple glazed. If such a window is a fixed component it is three-paned insulating glass with a ventilation shutter that can be opened. The shutter may also have an insect net.

Further information on the planning of sauna windows is given in Chapter 2.

Ventilation requires inlets and outlets for incoming and outgoing air. The fresh-air inlet in connection with the stove has a round vent of metal, elsewhere the inlets and outlets are closed with sliding wooden shutters. All inlets and outlets must be adjustable.

Flues and chimneys

A wood-fired stove requires a flue, which is built of brick or blocks according to the local regulations.

In a sauna of light construction at a holiday or summer home, the flue of the wood-fired stove can be built of industrially produced elements and units which are assembled according to the maker's instructions.

In most cases, the smallest diameter, width of the side or other transverse dimension of the flue is 100 mm. The damper is located in the flue 1600–1800 mm from floor level.

Flues and stoves are discussed in more detail in Chapter 5.

Table 1.
Properties of timber used in saunas.

Timber	spruce	pine	aspen	alder	birch	larch	oak	teak	mahogany
Botanical name	Picea abies	Pinus sylvestris	Populus tremula	Alnus glutinosa	Betula verrucosa	Larix sibirica	Quercus robur	Tectona grandis	Swietania macrophylla
density (kg/m^3)*	ca. 450	ca. 490	ca. 450	ca. 510	ca. 610	ca. 550	ca. 660	ca. 680	ca. 550
shrinkage (%) **									
–radial	ca. 3,6	ca. 4,0	ca. 3,5	ca. 4,4	ca. 5,3	ca. 5,4	ca. 4,3	ca. 2,6	ca. 3,7
–tangential	ca. 7,8	ca. 7,7	ca. 8,5	ca. 9,3	ca. 7,8	ca. 12,0	ca. 8,9	ca. 5,0	ca. 5,1
resin content	relatively resinous	resinous	–	–	–	Highly resinous	–	–	–
resistance to moisture	relatively poor	resistant heartwood	poor	poor	poor	good	good	good	good
scent	faint resin scent	strong resin scent	sour smell when wet	–	–	Pleasant scent when wet	sour smell when wet	leathery scent	–
colour	light	light surface, red-brown heartwood	from grey-white to light brown (greys with age)	from reddish light hue to red-brown	light yellowish colour	surface light brown, heartwood greenish brown	from light brown to dark brown	from golden brown to dark brown	grey surface, red-brown heartwood

*15 % humidity
** Shrinkage from fresh to completely dry.
The wood is easily warped if the difference between radial and tangential shrinkage is great (e.g. in larch).

Thermal conductivity is small and directly proportional to density. Thermal conductivity increases with the rise of humidity in the wood. The specific heat capacity of all types of timber listed here is small and almost the same: 1.34 kJ/(kg/ K) in an absolute dry state. The specific heat capacity of moist wood is estimated by summing the respective specific heat capacities of the wood when dry and that of the water (4.19 kJ/kg K) contained in it.

Linings and Cladding

The sauna

The following properties are required of lining materials in the stove room:
- low heat storage to prevent waste of heat in the heating of components and to prevent the surfaces from burning the skin.
- low thermal conductivity in surfaces adjacent to the sauna.
- good resistance to heat and moisture.
- the surfaces must be able to absorb and exude moisture.
- acoustic properties
- a pleasant scent and appearance

Timber is the material that conforms best to these requirements. It can be used to face all surfaces in the sauna within the bounds of fire-safety regulations. The grade of timber used for these purposes:
- must have few knots
- must exude little resin
- must be porous

Spruce with few knots is well suited for all surfaces in a sauna. A disadvantage of pine is the amount of resin in the wood.

Table 1 presents the properties of certain species of timber and Table 2 contains examples of their use in the sauna.

Chapter 4 discusses types of timber suitable for platforms and furnishings.

The linings of the walls and ceiling

Smooth planed boarding is a suitable lining material for the walls of the sauna. The ceiling is lined with smooth planed or sawn boarding. Lack of knots is an advantage in order to avoid drops of resin.

To minimize cracks caused by drying, the boards must be sufficiently thick in relation to their width. The scent of coniferous timber requires lining of sufficient thickness. Countersunk nails are recommended for the lining.

The exterior walls can have either vertical or horizontal cladding. The preservation of the water boarding requires that the moist air from the sauna is ventilated from beneath. Horizontal panelling is a better solution, since there will be a gap admitting air between the upright bottom battens and the parts behind the lining boards will be ventilated. It should also be remembered that in repairing the sauna it is easier to renew the lower horizontal boards. If a traditional vertical boarding is chosen, the supporting battens must have gaps for ventilation in a vertical direction. The wooden wall lining is not extended down to the floor.

The same boarding as in the walls or overlapping boards can be used for the ceiling. There should be a tight fit to prevent visible gaps and cracks when the boards move or possibly warp.

The area above a wood-fired stove must be protected in accordance with fire-safety regulations, for example with fibre cement. The permitted distances between the stove and other components are given in Chapter 5.

Floor surfaces

As the temperature at floor level in a sauna rarely rises above 30 °C, normal lining materials for damp conditions can be used. The floor area around a wood-fired stove must have a non-inflammable surface.

If there is thermal insulation in the floor, the surface material must be waterproof, or the underlying component must be insulated against moisture from above with a water-proofing

Table 2.
The uses of different types of timber in the sauna.

	Stove room				Washing room		
	interior lining	floors	platform framework	doors and windows	interior lining	floors	doors and windows
spruce	•	•	•	•	•	•	•
pine	•	•	•	•	•	•	•
larch	(•)	(•)			(•)		
teak		•				•	•

membrane. A waterproof surfacing material that can also be used in this connection is a plastic mat with welded seams. If such is used, a water-proofing membrane is not necessary. The plastic mat must extend to a minimum of 100 mm against the walls.

A concrete floor is usually covered with ceramic tiles. The floor tiles should have coarse or studded surfaces to prevent slipping.

The floors in the sauna are inclined to conduct water towards a drain. The minimum gradients of the floor are as follows:
- wooden floor 1:30
- tiled floor 1:100
- floor with plastic mat 1:100

Protection of surfaces

Timber in the sauna is susceptible to damage, discoloration and rot caused by moisture. The components and details of the sauna must be planned to withstand a moderate degree of damp without protective treatment. Sufficient ventilation and proper airing after the bath facilitate the drying of wooden surfaces and their preservation. The components beneath surfaces and the details of the interior should be made so as to avoid unventilated or poorly ventilated conditions, which will cause damage. The wooden parts of saunas which are in continuous use over long periods come into contact with a great deal of moisture and require protective measures.

To facilitate the cleaning, the lining of the sauna walls and ceiling and the wooden doors and window frames can be treated with special protective substance designed for use in saunas. Depending on use, the treatment is repeated once a year or every few years.

Fig. 57. If the walls and floor are of masonry, wooden ceiling materials and linings will reduce noise.

The unplastered brick surfaces in the sauna are left untreated. Plastered surfaces are faced with ceramic tiles or painted with heat-resistant paint according to the manufacturer's instructions.

Steel and metal surfaces are treated with rust-proofing paint and painted twice with alkyd paint.

The surfaces of a sauna interior must withstand heat and moisture. Surfaces in contact with the skin of the bathers must not become too hot, nor aggravate the skin. Materials should not issue unpleasant odours.

The washing room

Wall and ceiling linings

Wood panels, ceramic wall tiles, high-pressure laminate boards and other moisture-resistant cladding materials can be used in the washing room, in addition to painting the masonry surfaces.

The wooden lining must have a ventilated gap at least 20 mm thick behind it. Galvanized or copper nails are to be used. Countersunk nails are used in flush nailing.

A masonry wall is the best base for affixing ceramic tiles. Building board is used in the tiling of a wood framework wall. Suitable board or sheet materials are gypsum and fibre cement. The rear side of the tiles is insulated against moisture. Waterproof mortar is used to cement the tiles in place.

The laminate board is nailed to the wooden wall framework according to the maker's instructions. A ventilated gap is required between a masonry wall and the laminate board.

Plastic-coated wall materials are glued according to the manufacturer's instructions. The seams and joins with other components must be carefully sealed with flexible sealant. The surfacing material must extend at least 20 mm onto the floor and under the batten of the door frame.

The washing room ceiling can have the same lining as the stove room ceiling. Where the walls and floor are of masonry, a wooden lining on the ceiling reduces noise.

Floors

The floors of the washing room are finished in the same manner as in the stove room.

Protective measures

The wooden wall and ceiling linings of the washing room and its windows and doors are to be treated twice with protective materials.

The plastered, concrete and metal surfaces of the washing room are treated as in the stove room.

The dressing room

Wall and ceiling lining

The wall and ceiling lining of the dressing room can be the same as in normal dwelling rooms. The walls can be covered, for example, with moisture-resistant fabric wallpaper, fabric coated board, or wooden panels. Wooden panels and acoustic ceiling board for dampening sound can be used for the ceiling.

Floors

All floor surfacing materials that can be used in normal dwelling rooms are suitable for the dressing room of the sauna. Natural-fibre coir or hemp matting can be used in the dressing rooms of privately used saunas.

Protective measures

The surfaces of the dressing room are treated as in dwelling rooms.

4. Platforms and Furnishings

This chapter discusses the design and construction of sauna platforms and the choice of materials. There are also instructions on fixtures and equipment for the washing and dressing rooms.

General Remarks

The shape of the platforms depends on the size, floor plan and use of the sauna. The platforms fall into four basic types according to shape and form. See Fig. 58.

The dimensioning of platforms and considerations for disabled bathers are presented in Chapter 2. The platforms of the smoke sauna are discussed in Chapter 7.

The Platforms

Framework and ledgers

Supporting structure

The sauna platform can be supported by the walls, the walls and floor, or solely by the floor with wood or steel stanchions. In small saunas the platforms are supported by the walls to facilitate cleaning. Accordingly, the walls are constructed from the outset to permit a solid support for the platforms.

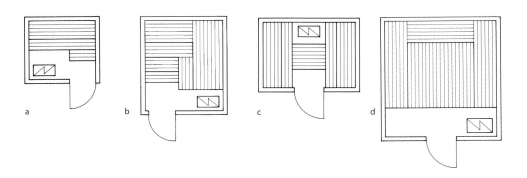

Fig. 58. Sauna platforms. a) straight platform, b) L-shaped layout, c) facing platforms d) U-shaped layout. Scale 1:100.

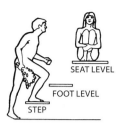

Fig. 59. Platform levels.

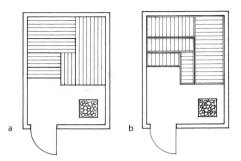

Fig. 60. The removable parts of the platforms can be built with the boarding placed transversely or lengthwise. Shown here are platforms in an L-shaped layout with a) lengthwise and b) transverse boarding. Scale 1:100.

Platforms borne by the floor are used in saunas whose wall construction cannot bear the resulting weight and in large saunas, for example for use by the public. The lower part of the platform can be filled and lined, for example, with ceramic tiles. See Fig. 63 c.

A straight platform supported by the wall is a structurally simple design. Platforms in L or U-shaped configuration will partly require support from the floor.

The step platform may be movable if it rests sturdily on the floor surface.

Wooden framework

The maximum lengthwise distance between wooden ledgers is 600 mm. The sizes of the supports are given in Table 3. The ledgers are placed on 45 x 70 mm transverse members affixed to the wall. A gap of 4–6 mm is left between the supports and the wall, for example with a piece of plywood placed in it.

Platforms supported by the floor are made of timber with minimum dimensions of 45 x 70 mm. The distance between the supports is defined by the span allowed by the ledgers. Smooth planed timber is used for the ledgers and the supports. Adjustable steel stanchions are placed in the bottom part of the floor supports.

The nails used in the platforms are to be of galvanized steel. The screws must be of brass or galvanized steel, and both nails and screws are to be countersunk. Wooden dowels or plugs are used on visible surfaces.

Steel framework

The ledgers and supports of the platforms can be made of galvanized or stainless steel, for example with 60 x 40mm tubing of rectangular section with a wall thickness of 2–3 mm depending on the span. The steel ledgers are joined to the

Table 3.
Relationship of ledgers to span in wooden platform constructions.

Span	Ledger size
< 2000 mm	45 x 95 mm
2000–2500 mm	45 x 100 mm
2500–3000 mm	45 x 145 mm

wall, for example with supports of steel plate. Fig. 62.

The floor supports are made of similar tubing as the ledgers. The joins are accordingly welded. The maximum distance between floor supports is 2500 mm. Adjustable steel stanchions can be used to compensate for the slope of the floor.

Platforms

The platforms are made of smooth planed timber. The seat parts and footrests must always be removable. To facilitate cleaning, the various parts are divided into parts that can be removed by one person. Small seat parts can be attached with hinges onto the rear wall.

The seat platforms are made timber with low heat storage properties, e.g. spruce with few knots or aspen. Spruce with few knots is the best type of timber for the Finnish sauna; a disadvantage of pine is its high resin content. Teak can be used in saunas which are in active use, such as public saunas. It has good moisture-resistance properties, but tends to become hot.

Fig. 61. The verge boards are separated from the framework with pieces of plywood. The platform boards are affixed with the inner side facing upwards. Photo: Rauno Träskelin.

Fig. 62. Steel ledger joined to the wall. View from below. Photo: Rauno Träskelin.

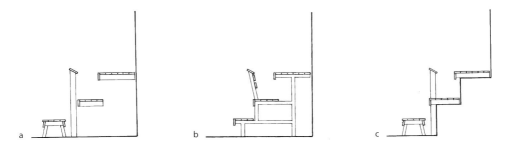

Fig. 63. The supports of the platforms and their construction can be designed in various ways: a) supported by the wall, b) supported from floor level with steel structures, c) fixed, water-proofed platform construction. Scale 1:50.

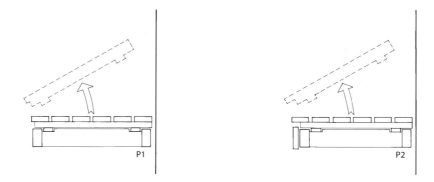

Fig. 64. Lengthwise boarding in a platform with wooden ledgers. Scale 1:20. Details shown in Fig. 68.

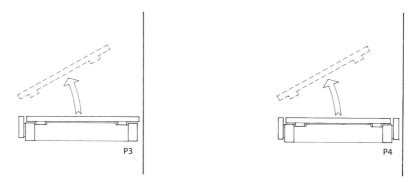

Fig. 65. Transverse boarding in a platform with wooden ledgers. Scale 1:20. Details shown in Fig. 69.

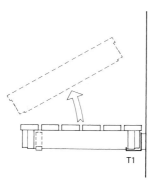 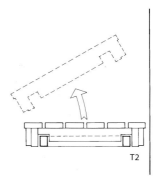

Fig. 66. Platform with steel supports. Scale 1:20. Details shown in Fig. 70.

Fig. 67. Platform with supports of steel tubing. Scale 1:20. Details shown in Fig. 71.

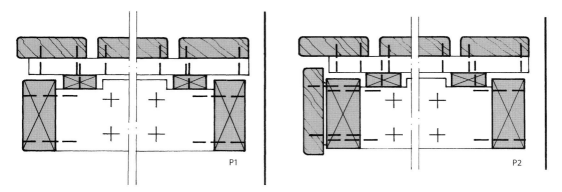

Fig. 68. Lengthwise boarding of a platform with wooden ledgers, details. Scale 1:5.

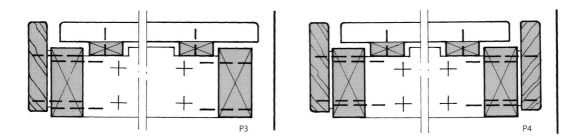

Fig. 69. Transverse boarding of a platform with wooden ledgers, details. Scale 1:5.

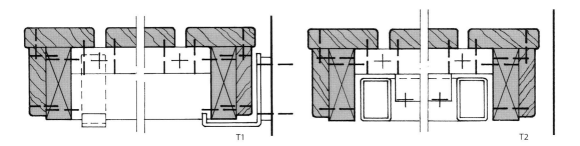

Fig. 70. Platform with steel supports, details. Scale 1:5.

Fig. 71. Platform with supports of steel tubing. Scale 1:5.

Fig. 72. The seat and foot platforms are to be removable. Photo: Rauno Träskelin.

Fig. 73. The railing is usually made to also serve as a footrest. Photo: Rauno Träskelin.

Table 4.
Timber suitable for sauna platforms and furnishings

	platforms	washing room furnishings
spruce	•	•
pine	(•)	•
larch	(•)	
aspen	•	
alder	•	(•)
birch		(•)
teak	(•)	•

Examples of timber for platforms and furnishings are given in Table 4. Types of timber suitable for sauna components and linings and their properties are discussed in Chapter 3. Domestic species of wood are recommended for the Finnish sauna.

The platform boards are usually 22 or 28 mm thick and 95 or 120 mm wide. The edges of the upper surface are bevelled. The boards are spaced with ca. 10 mm gaps between them and they are screwed from beneath onto the transverse supports (28 x 95 mm).

The maximum distance between the transverse supports is 600 mm. Battens (28 x 28 mm) can be affixed to the transverse supports to keep the removable seat parts in place. The platforms are placed at a distance of 20–30 mm from the wall.

Railings and banisters

A sturdy railing is built around the stove to prevent the bathers from falling onto it and also to serve as a footrest, Fig. 73. It should include a lower rail element for children. The railing can be made of wood or steel faced with wood. It is joined to the walls and supported from the floor and ceiling. If more than two steps are needed for access to the platform, there should be a handrail joined to the floor or wall, which is built in the same way as the railing around the stove. In saunas for disabled persons, there should be a handrail on both sides of the steps. The handrail is to be designed to provide a sturdy grip.

Backrests

There should also be backrests in connection with the platforms. These are usually made of the same timber as the platforms. An example of a backrest is given in Fig. 74.

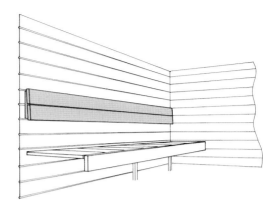

Fig. 74. Backrest.

Furnishings and Equipment

Table 5 (p. 68) lists furnishings and equipment for the stove room, dressing room and washing room of the sauna. Furnishings and equipment for stove rooms, washing rooms, dressing rooms in saunas for the disabled are discussed in Chapter 2.

The stove room

In addition to the platforms, the stove room requires a bench on the floor for children, the elderly and the disabled.

A summer sauna without a separate washing room requires an additional bench 400–500 mm high and 400–500 mm wide. The length of the bench is selected according to the dimensions of the room. The timber is usually the same as that used for the platforms. The legs of the bench can be of wood or metal and are fitted with rubber doorstops.

Fig. 75. Removable headrests can also be placed on the platform. The Finnish Sauna Society.

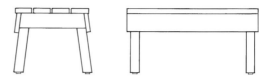

Fig. 76. Sauna bench. Scale 1:20.

Wooden duckboards can be used in saunas with uninsulated masonry floors. These can be made, for example, of 21 x 45 mm battens spaced at 5 mm intervals. Rubber stops are nailed or screwed to the lower surface to facilitate drying. The duckboards should be raised during cleaning.

Separate inclined headrests of wood (size 300 x 400 mm) can also be used on the platforms. These can be made, for example, of 28 x 95 mm boards, Fig. 75.

The washing room

There can also be duckboards similar to those in the stove room on the washing room floor. Wooden or plastic stools or benches are suitable for the washing room. There can also be a fixed bench laid with ceramic tiles, with a removable duckboard on top of it. There must also be shelving for washing gear and pegs for towels in the washing room.

In public saunas, partitions can be installed between the showers. The showers are fitted with soap-holders and soap and shampoo dispensers.

The dressing room

The furnishings of the dressing room are selected according to the character of the room.

The dressing room is fitted with benches, a table, pegs, shelves, a mirror and a coat rack. 600 mm of bench space is reserved per bather.

In public saunas the bathers store their clothes usually in lockers, for which 400–500 mm of space are reserved per bather. Space is also required for hair-dryers and drinks machines.

Fig. 77. a), b). Examples of dressing room furnishings and lockers. a) Photo Teemu Töyrylä.

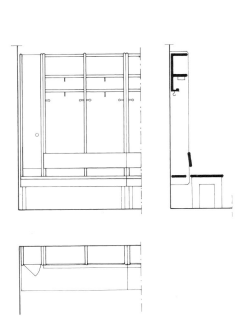

Fig. 78. Examples of storage space for clothes. Scale 1:50.

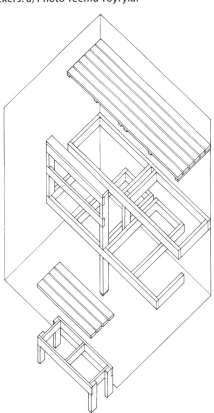

Fig. 79. Straight platform construction of wood. Scale 1:50.

PLATFORMS AND FURNISHINGS

Table 5.
Furnishings and equipment for the stove room, washing room and dressing room.

		Holiday (summer) sauna without washing room	Holiday (summer) sauna with washing room	Holiday sauna (year-round) or sauna in an outbuilding	Block sauna	Home sauna	Apartment sauna	Public sauna
Sauna	wooden duckboard	•	•	•	•	•	•	(•)
	separate bench	•						
	wooden headrest	(•)	(•)	(•)		(•)	(•)	
	scoop etc. for throwing water	•	•	•	•	•	•	•
	thermometer	(•)	(•)	•	•	•	•	•
Washing	wooden duckboard		•	•	(•)	•	•	(•)
	stool		(•)	(•)	(•)	(•)	(•)	(•)
	bench		•	•	•	•	•	•
	shelves		•	•	•	•	•	•
	towel pegs		•	•	•	•	•	•
	shower partitions							•
	soap holders				•	•	•	•
	soap dispensers							•
Dressing	benches			•	•	•		•
	table			•	•	•		•
	clothes pegs			•	•	•		•
	lockers							•
	shelves			•	•	•		•
	mirror			•	•	•		•
	hair-dryer							•
	wastebasket			•	•	•		•
	laundry basket							•

5. Sauna Stoves

This chapter presents Finnish stove models presently in use. The stoves of the smoke sauna are presented in Chapter 7. The heating of the sauna and related energy requirements are discussed in Chapter 6.

General Remarks

The stove is such an important part of the Finnish sauna that it has been called the heart of the sauna.

The purpose of the stove is to heat the sauna and to produce hot vapour (Fi. löyly). The effectivity of the stove in this respect is dependent on the number of stones in it. When water is thrown on the stones the temperature in the stove room usually goes down, although the opposite is felt by the bather because of the increase in humidity.

The kind of hot vapour obtained depends on the interior climate of the sauna and its various factors: air temperature and humidity, radiated heat from the stove and the interior surfaces, ventilation, purity of the air, and its ion content. Further factors are the composition of the stones, their condition and temperature. More details on the interior climate of the sauna are given in Chapter 6.

Stove types presently in use can be classed as in Fig. 80. In a heat-storage stove, the stones are heated to the desired temperature before bathing. There is no heating during the actual bathing. A continuous burning stove is heated prior to bathing and during it.

Thermal energy for the stoves is mainly provided by wood fuel or electricity, but also by bottled or natural gas and oil. Electrically heated stoves are usually of the continuous heating type, whereas those heated with wood, gas or oil can be of both types. The generally small electric stove does not require a flue.

All stove types are available factory-made. The flueless smoke stove and the wood-fired heat-storage stove can be constructed in situ

Shown in Fig. 82 is a heat-storage model wood-fired stove of brick.

Wood-fired Stoves

The smoke stove

The smoke stove is the oldest stove type. It was originally a setting of stones with a fire space inside it.

The smoke stove has a flueless fireplace in which the flames heat the stones above the fire space. The resulting smoke is led out of the sauna via a ventilation outlet and the door. The sauna itself is heated by the hot smoke and thermal radiation from the stones. The air in the sauna has a slight smell of smoke.

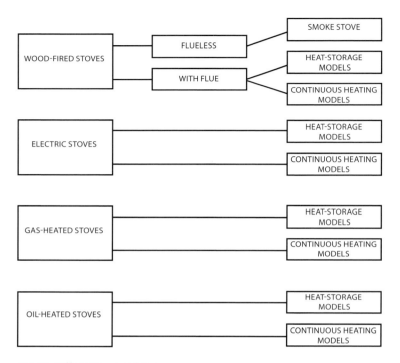

Fig. 80. Different types of stoves.

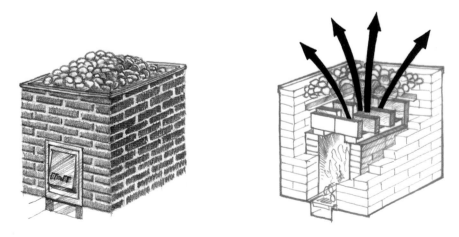

Fig. 81. Smoke stove of brick.

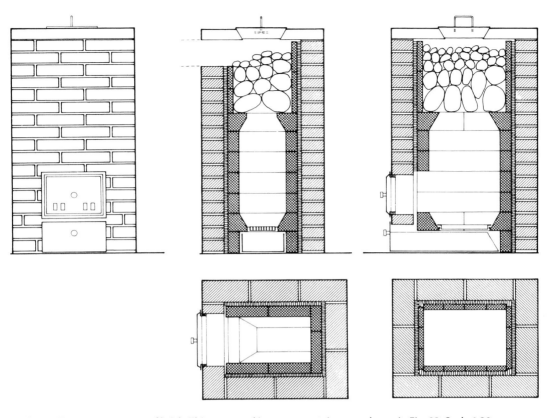

Fig. 82. Heat-storage stove of brick. This stove and its water container are shown in Fig. 92. Scale 1:20.

A smoke stove requires a relatively large number of stones (120 kg or more). The amount of stones should be in proportion to the volume of the stove room and the bathing habits of its users. A smoke sauna takes 2–4 hours to heat.

The masonry and brickwork, properties and heating of the smoke stove are discussed in more detail in Chapter 7.

The heat-storage stove

A flued stove has been developed from the smoke stove, in which the stones are in a closed space with a lid. The flames and smoke pass through the stones into the flue. This stove type can also be used in the manner of a smoke stove by closing the smoke damper and by opening the lid over the stones.

When this type of stove is used, the sauna is heated with the aid of hot air flowing throw the space reserved for the stones. The temperature is adjusted with the lid covering the stones.

The amount of stones depends on the degree to which the sauna is used. A smaller amount of stones (35–120 kg in family saunas depending

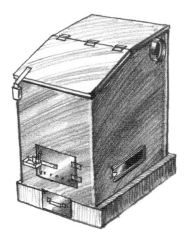

Fig. 83. Wood-fired heat-storage stove.

Fig. 84. Wood-fired continuous heating stove.

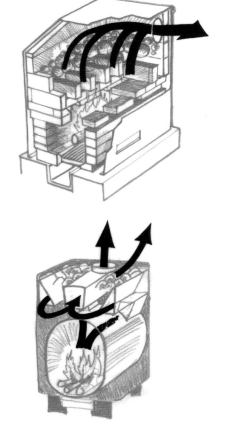

on capacity and model; up to 650 kg in public saunas) is required than in the smoke stove, for the stones retain their heat for a long time in the closed compartment. A smaller amount of stones also means shorter heating time (1–2 hrs).

As the space for the stones is insulated and can be closed off, it is possible to ventilate the sauna during the bathing and the bathers can also wash themselves in the stove room.

The continuous heating stove

In the continuous heating stove the flames are usually led via metal ducts among the stones and beneath them before passing on to the flue.

This stove type is heated during the bathing. The sauna is heated by hot air circulating among the stones and in the ducts of the metal casing of the stove. The temperature is regulated with the amount of fuel and the speed of combustion.

A smaller amount of stones is required than in the heat-storage type: 25–100 kg depending on capacity and model. The stove takes approximately half an hour to heat.

As the stones are not in contact with the fire they will not become sooty and the air in the sauna remains pure.

There is often a water heater attached to the side of the stove or connected to the flue. In some saunas there is also a humidifier.

Electrically Heated Sauna Stoves

Continuous heating models

The electric sauna stove is usually of the continuous heating type. The stones are heated by elements placed beneath, among and around the stones. The sauna gains its heat from air passing through the stove. The temperature is regulated by an element control unit and a thermostat.

There is usually a small amount of stones (3–40 kg in a family sauna depending on capacity and model; up to 150 kg in a public sauna). Heating time is approximately 30 minutes. The stones do not gather soot.

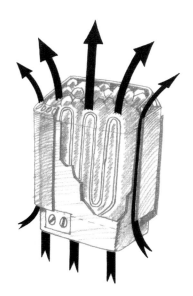

Fig. 85. Continuous heating electric stove.

A continuous heating electric stove can also be of lamellar form (Fig. 86).

The energy requirements and installation of electric stoves are discussed in Chapter 6.

Heat-storage models

An electrically heated stove can also be of the heat-storage type, in which case it will have more stones than the continuous heating type and the casing is usually thermally insulated. The stones can also be heated with elements, in which case the heating resistors are encased in elements of ceramic material. This stove type takes 1–1.5 hours to heat.

A heat-storage electric stove can be left in a stand-by state, in which the stones are kept at a temperature of 200–300 °C under the lid. When the bathing begins, the temperature is raised, the lid is opened and water is thrown on the stones.

Other Stove Types

Oil-heated stoves

Oil-heated stoves can be of the heat-storage or continuous heating type.

The pressure burner is located in a completely enclosed space in the bottom part of the stove. The burner space is ventilated from outside. It is not necessary to construct a separate room for the burner. Local safety regulations and the manufacturer's instructions must be followed when installing oil-heated stoves.

Oil-heated stoves are exceptionally used, for example, in public saunas.

Protective Measures

Local safety regulations and the manufacturer's instructions must be followed when installing stoves.

Fig. 86. Wall-model electric stove of lamellar design. The heating elements are encased in stone blocks.

Fig. 87. Heat-storage electric stove kept at basic temperature for immediate use.

Wood-fired stoves

The necessary distances between wood-fired stoves and inflammable components are listed in Table 6.

A single light protective barrier can be made from the following:

- non-inflammable fibre-reinforced cement board (minimum thickness 7 mm)
- calcium silicate board (minimum thickness 7 mm)
- hot galvanized sheet metal (minimum thickness 1 mm) affixed at 40–50 cm intervals

A light double barrier can be made from two of the above-mentioned.

A ventilation gap of at least 30 mm is to be left between the protective boards and the surface to be protected. To ensure ventilation the edge must be free of the floor and the ceiling.

Corresponding to a single light barrier is brickwork of a minimum thickness of 55 mm which is left unfaced at the sides and placed at a minimum distance of 30 mm from the surface that is to be protected. Brickwork 110 mm in thickness and placed 30 mm from the surface concerned corresponds to a light double protective barrier.

The construction of a light barrier is presented in Figs. 88 and 89.

The inflammable floor surface in front of the fire chamber is protected with sheet metal joined tightly to the floor and the stove. With a fire

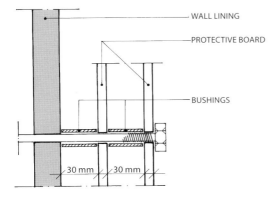

Fig. 88. Light double barrier fixed in place.

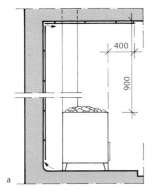
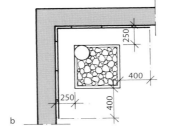
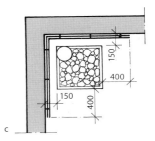

Fig. 89. Light barriers for sauna stoves: a) and b) light single barrier, c) light double barrier.

Table 6.
Required distances of wood-fired stoves from inflammable components according to Finnish regulations. Local safety regulations and the manufacturer's instructions must be followed when installing stoves.

Front	1000 mm	Distance can be decreased by 50% with a light single barrier and by 75% with a light double barrier.
Rear	500 mm	
Sides	500 mm	
Bottom	250 mm	Distance can be decreased by 25% with a light single barrier and by 50% with a light double barrier.
Top	1200 mm	

A space measuring one metre must be left free in front of the stove for tending the fire.

chamber fitted with a door the protected area must extend to a minimum of 100 mm on both sides of the door and 400 mm in front of it.

The required distances around factory-made wood-fired stoves must be marked on a plate affixed by the maker on the stove.

Electrically heated stoves

Current safety regulations and the manufacturer's instructions must be followed when installing electric stoves of under 20 kW. The instructions must list required distances from the upper surface of the stove to the ceiling, from the bottom surface to the floor, distances from the front surface to the platform or protective railing, and the distances from the side and ear walls. It is not permissible to make exceptions to the stated distances from inflammable components, for example by installing protective boards or light barriers not included in the construction of the stove.

The minimum height of the stove room varies according to the stove, but it must not be less than 1900 mm. Where the controls are an integral part of the stove, the stove must be installed to leave them visible and to permit their use. For example, there can be an unrestricted space of 800 mm in front of the controls.

Separately installed stove controls require a free area of 800 mm.

Oil-heated stoves

The walls and ceiling components in saunas with oil-heated stoves must be protected as stated in the regulations concerning woodfired stoves.

Flues

The fireplace and the chimney are built on a fixed non-inflammable foundation. The masonry and brickwork are moisture-proofed from the foundation, for example with asphalted felt.

The sauna stove usually has a half-brick flue, Fig. 90.

With a suitable degree of porosity, burnt brick is a good material for the chimney. Accordingly, changes in humidity in the flue will not affect the draught.

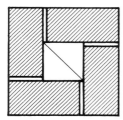

Fig. 90. Half-brick flue.

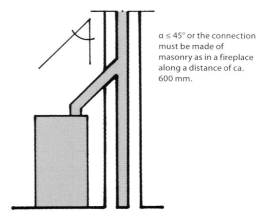

Fig. 91. Connection of a metal stove.

The chimney is made of weather-resistant, exterior quality perforated brick of basic or normal size using weather-proof cement grout or gauged mortar. Inside the sauna, so-called basic-sized solid brick can also be used below the thermal insulation of the roof-space. In the interior, and particularly in the lower part of the chimney, loam mortar of sufficient flexibility to withstand the thermal expansion caused by the exhaust gases is to be used. As this mortar is soft, the visible parts should have recessed joints which are finished in the later stages of the bricklaying.

The temperature of the exhaust gases from may exceed 350 °C. To prevent damage to the flue, the passage of the exhaust gases must be facilitated and sharp turnings or angles must be avoided. If the connection to the flue is at a sharper angle than 45°, the flue is regarded as a continuation of the actual fireplace, which requires the use of fire-proof materials, Fig. 91.

To prevent damage caused by rainwater, the chimney must always have a covering of concrete or a removable piece of sheet metal.

The flue can also be constructed of elements. Available for this purpose are series of fire-proof flue elements and expanded clay aggregate blocks. Metal flues are also in use. Owing

Fig. 92. Stove shown in Fig. 82 with hot-water container joined to the same flue. Photo: Rauno Träskelin.

SAUNA STOVES | 77

to their light weight, flues of elements and metal parts are usually installed in the saunas of holiday homes. Local regulations must be followed when planning and constructing flues.

The Stove Stones

Certain properties are required of the heat stones of the stove, and different rocks vary greatly in this respect. These differences result from the fact that different rocks are composed of different minerals. The properties of good stove stones are listed in Table 8. Table 7 gives instructions on the use of stove stones.

Dark intrusive rocks consisting of heavy minerals are suitable for the sauna stove. These include the following:

- peridotite
- olivine
- pyroxenite
- hornblendite
- perknite
- diabase
- chromite
- norite
- gabro

But even these rocks do not have suitable properties in all respects. One of the most common problems is the presence of ferric sulphides (pyrites) which release sulphuric oxide and sulphuric acid into the ambient atmosphere when the stones become worn.

Ceramic and steatite stove stones are also available.

The Heating of Wood-fired Stoves

The fire chamber should be emptied before lighting the fire. The accumulation of ashes prevents air from circulating and cooling the grate, which will lead to damage.

Dry firewood is placed in the chamber and lit in the centre. The firewood should be stacked with gaps to permit the passage of air through the grate into the fire. The damper should be completely open during the heating.

If the sauna has not been heated for a long time, care must be taken when beginning the heating.

In the initial stage, as much air as possible should be let into the fire chamber. When the firewood has ignited, the intake of air is regulated so that the fire burns briskly with a slight rushing noise. The intake of air is regulated with the shutter of the fire chamber and its vents.

When half the firewood has burned, the fire chamber is filled as many times as required for heating.

Wood-fired continuous heating stoves

Continuous heating stoves are heated during the actual bathing. The bathing can commence when the stones are hot enough to produce vapour. The stones are not heated to a red glow.

Wood-fired heat-storage stoves

In the last stages of the heating, small pieces of firewood of even size are placed in the fire chamber, after which the shutters, vents and the damper are closed.

The heating may end when the lower parts of the uppermost stones glow red. The heating must continue until soot and tar have burnt from the stones, thus permitting clean vapour.

Finally, water is thrown on the stones with the damper completely open to lead dust and ashes from the stones into the flue. The damper is then closed, the lid over the stones is opened, and the sauna bath may commence.

Table 7.
Instructions concerning stove stones.

Heat-storage stoves	Continuous heating stoves
Place large stones on the bottom and small stones on top for even heating.	Use stones of the same size to provide good heat transmission and circulation of air.
The stones must be washed prior to installing.	
Gradual increase of heat preserves the stones and conserves energy.	
Hot water thrown on the stones leads to slower wear on the stones than using cold water.	
Rearrange the stones at sufficient intervals, e.g. every 200-300 heating hours, to ensure good air circulation.	
Even good stones will disintegrate. Inspect the stones yearly and replace them at sufficient intervals.	

Table 8.
Properties of stove stones.

Advantages	Corresponding rock types
non-polluting (no emission of hazardous gases or dust)	non-sulphide (non-pyritic) and **non-asbestos** rocks consisting of silicates and oxides.
high thermal capacity (particularly in heatstorage stoves)	dark, heavy rocks, especially types consisting of olivine, pyroxines and ferric and chrome oxides.
high degree of thermal conductivity (particularly in continuous heating stoves)	dense, non-porous rocks
low and even thermal expansion	no major differences; rocks of even colour are usually best.
low degree of cracking	fine-structured, resilient rocks and those of **flaky soft minerals**
chemical durability (non-weathering, no chemical disintegration of minerals)	non-sulphide and non-carbonate rocks, especially those consisting of OH silicates (e.g. amphiboles) and oxides.

6. The Design of Heating, Plumbing, Ventilation and Electrical Installations for the Sauna

This chapter is on the planning and design of heating, plumbing, ventilation and electrical installations for the sauna. The section on heating, plumbing and ventilation discusses the properties and values required of the inner climate of the sauna. There are also instructions on defining the specific heating requirements and on ventilation systems. The section on electrical installations describes current requirements and also gives instructions for the lighting of saunas. Electric stoves are also discussed in Chapter 5.

General Remarks

Ventilation and heating are used to:
- maintain a pleasant interior climate for bathing in the sauna
- dry the sauna rooms after the bath
- prevent the decay or corrosion of components and equipment

Ventilation also ensures the proper intake of air required by the stove.

The following requirements are placed on the inner climate of the stove room:
- air temperature of 70–100 °C at head level
- humidity between 40–70 g of vapour per kilogram of air
- even heat radiation from all directions
- temperature of interior location above the platforms should be close to that of the air.

The recommended properties for the washing room are:
- air temperature 22–25 °C
- maximum relative humidity 60%
- minimum surface temperature of floor 23 °C

Dressing room:
- air temperature 22–25 °C
- maximum relative humidity 60%
- minimum surface temperature of floor 21 °C

In rooms for bare-footed use the surface temperatures of the floor should correspond to the recommendations given in Table 9.

Table 9.
Recommended surface temperatures in rooms for bare-footed use

Floor surface	Temperature
stone, concrete	27...30 °C
linoleum, PVC	25...29 °C
wood, cork	23...28 °C
textiles	21...28 °C

Q = heat requirement MJ
A = wall area m²
t = bathing time (h)

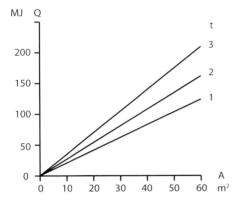

Fig. 93. Heating requirements using a wood-fired continuous heating stove with heating begun at +20°C. 1.7 MJ per bather is added to the recommended value. If the heating is begun at -20°C, the heating requirement will be 1.5 times as great.

P = maximum output of stove kW
A = wall area m²

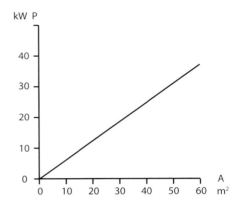

Fig. 94. Heating requirements using a wood-fired heat-storage stove with heating begun at +20° C. 1.7 MJ per bather is added to the recommended value. If heating is begun at -20°C, the heating requirement will be 1.5 times as great.

Heating

Outside the times set apart for bathing, the various parts of the sauna are kept at room temperature with radiators, electric, floor or air heating. The sauna can also be kept at room temperature by using an electric stove producing a low temperature.

Floor heating is recommended as it increases comfort and helps to dry the sauna rooms. Floor heating should not, however, require differences in elevation among rooms and thus obstruct movement.

In a summer sauna, the washing and dressing rooms can be heated with the fireproof wall of the stove room. A large dressing or cooling room in intermittent use can have a heat-storage fireplace or an ordinary fireplace, and in addition some other heating device.

For the bath, the sauna is heated with the stove. The heating requirements of a wood-fired heat-storage stove can be estimated from the table given in Fig. 93. The corresponding requirements for continuous heating stoves are shown in Fig. 94. The relationship of the capacity of an electric stove to the volume of the stove room is discussed in the section on the selection of electric stoves.

Water Supply and Drains

The water supply and drains of the sauna are connected to the water mains and drains of

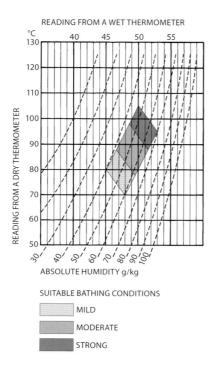

Fig. 95. Temperature and humidity conditions in a Finnish sauna at head height.

ly into a lake or river. In settled areas with no sewer system it is usually forbidden to drain water directly onto the surface of the ground. The water from the sauna must led via a cesspool into open ditches or a closed reservoir that can be emptied. In areas with zoning and building regulations and local plans concerning shore areas, special regulations are laid down concerning sewers.

Ventilation

In home and apartment saunas, air intakes and outlets are usually connected to the ventilation system of the building. Depending on times of use, block and public saunas should have a separate ventilation system serving only the sauna unit.

In mechanical intake and exhaust systems and in mechanical exhaust ventilation, the incoming air can be led to the location best suited to the specific conditions for bathing, i.e. near the ceiling at a minimum height of 500 mm above the stove. However, if natural ventilation is used, the location of the air intake vent has a great effect on the ventilation of the stove room.

For fire-safety reason, cold outside air should not be led directly to the bottom part of the electric stove, especially if the sensing element of the controls or limiting device is located in the stove itself.

Natural ventilation

Natural ventilation is suited to summer saunas with wood-fired stoves and no major requirements on the control or energy needs of ventilation.

the building in which it is located. The necessary number of showers and water outlets is discussed in Chapter 2.

The washing room must always have a floor drain. Owing to the risk that the water trap will dry, a floor drain is usually not installed in the stove room. The floor of the stove room is inclined towards the washing room. If a floor drain is installed in the stove room, a dry model must be used, connected to the floor drain of the washing room.

It is not permitted to lead waste water direct-

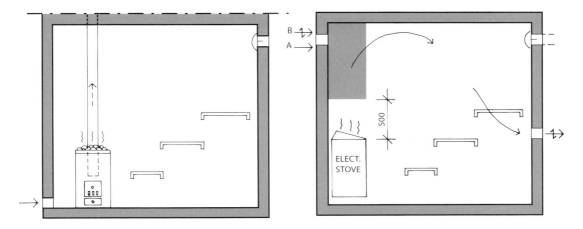

Fig. 96. Natural ventilation is suited to summer saunas with wood-fired stoves. The exhaust vent is usually kept shut during the bath and opened afterwards.

Fig. 97. Mechanical ventilation, a) exhaust, b) mechanical intake and exhaust system. Exhaust vent in the upper part is used only for drying the sauna. The intake vent is located in the area above the stove (marked in the drawing).

Air from outside is led via inlets or shutters in connection with the windows. The ventilation is effected by the difference in air pressure caused by the difference between exterior and interior temperature.

The exhaust vent is usually kept closed during the bath and opened afterwards.

Ventilation of the stove room

Air from outside is led into the lower part of the stove room via an adjustable inlet located near the stove.

If the air is led out of the stove room directly through the wall, the outlet should be placed high on the wall, Fig. 96. A location close to the stove should be avoided. The openings of the ventilators should be larger than 300 cm^2.

If the exhaust air is led into a duct above the roof, the area of the adjustable intake should be approximately 25 cm^2 per bather, and a minimum of 75 cm^2. The outlet should have an area of 30 cm^2 per bather, however a minimum outlet area of 150 cm^2 is required.

If the stove room is also used for washing, an adjustable intake is recommended at a low location near the washing area, permitting its cooling if necessary.

Ventilation of the washing and dressing rooms

The washing and dressing rooms are to have adjustable intakes placed near the floor. The required area is 25 cm^2 per person (minimum 100 cm^2). There must also be an adjustable outlet near the ceiling of 50 cm^2 per person (minimum 200 cm^2).

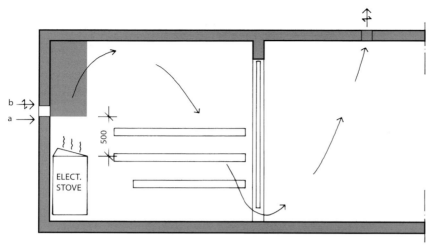

Fig. 98. A small sauna with exhaust air led out from under a door without a treshold. a) mechanical exhaust, b) mechanical intake and exhaust.

Mechanical ventilation

Stove room

The intake air of the stove room is usually led directly from the outside. The intake is located at a minimum height of 500 mm above the stove in the wall or ceiling to prevent draughts or cold downward draught onto the floor. If the outside air is led via a duct through other rooms, the duct must be thermally insulated. The recommended place for the outlet is below platform level, Fig. 97.

In small saunas, as in apartments, the exhaust air from the stove room can also be led under a door without a threshold into the washing room, Fig. 98.

Ventilation of the washing and dressing rooms

The air entering the washing room comes from the outside and from the stove room and dressing room. The outside air is led via an intake or shutter in connection with a window located above the heating radiator. If the outside air is led through other rooms, the duct requires thermal insulation.

The exhaust air of the washing room is led into the duct system from above the showers and via a separate WC in connection with the washing room. The WC has lower air pressure in relation to the washing room, and the washing is similarly sub-pressurized in relation to the other rooms.

Outside air is led into the dressing room, the intake being arranged as in the washing room.

The exhaust air of the dressing room is partly led into exhaust air ducts. Part of the air is led out via a WC in connection with the room and via the washing room.

Mechanical intake and exhaust ventilation

In a mechanical ventilation system the intake air from outside is heated before being led into the sauna.

In an air heating system (i.e. mechanized ventilation connected to air heating equipment) the mixture of outside air and recirculated and return air is heated before being led into the sauna.

Mechanical ventilation combined with air heating permits the recovery of exhaust air and the heating of intake air, whereby the ventilation conserves energy, does not produce draughts and can be controlled.

Ventilation of the stove room

In a mechanical system the intake air of the stove room is heated outside air. The intake vent is placed in the ceiling or wall at a minimum height of 500 mm above the stove. If the duct from outside passes through other rooms, thermal insulation is required. The exhaust outlet is located below the seat level of the platforms, Fig. 97.

In small saunas, for example in apartments, the exhaust air of the stove room can be led out from under the washroom door if it has no threshold, Fig. 98.

In public saunas, part of the exhaust air is led directly from the sauna, and part of it exits via the washing room.

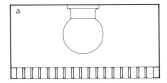
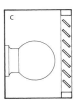 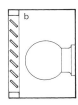

Fig. 99. Glare shields. a) Ceiling light with slats pointing directly downwards, b) in the upper part of the wall the slats are directed upwards, c) in the lower part and to the sides of the platform the slats are turned downwards.

Fig. 100. An example of lighting in a sauna. Photo: SunSauna.

Fig. 101. An example of lighting in a sauna. Photo: Mina Jokivirta.

Fig. 102. Lighting in a dressing room. Design by Interior Architects Sistem Ltd.

Ventilation of washing and dressing rooms

In mechanical systems, the intake air of the washing room is heated outside air, and also air from the stove room and dressing room. The flow of incoming air should be directed towards the windows to keep them dry and unmisted.

The exhaust air of the washing room is led into the ducts from above the showers and through a separate WC in connection with the washing room. The WC has lower air pressure in relation to the washing room, and the washing is similarly sub-pressurized in relation to the other rooms.

The intake air of the dressing room is heated outside air. The flow of incoming air should be directed away from the seats and benches. If the dressing room has a fireplace, the air required by the fire should be provided with a separate intake duct.

The exhaust air of the dressing room is led partly into the outlet ducts, and the remainder is led via a WC in connection with the dressing room and washing room.

Lighting

The sauna windows are discussed in Chapter 2.

The lighting of a sauna must be dim yet suffi-

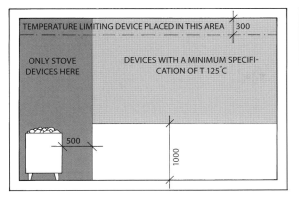 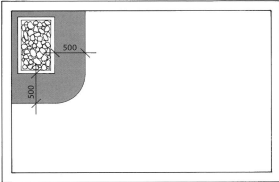

Fig. 103. Locations of electrical devices in the sauna according to Finnish regulations. Local regulations and instructions must be followed.

cient to ensure safe movement. Electric lighting can be varied with the location, type and power of the fitting. In placing the light fittings and directing the light, the upper part of the sauna and the seat level of the platforms should remain in darkness, but the steps and route of access should be lit. In selecting the location of the fitting, the need to change light bulbs without obstacles should also be taken into consideration.

Satisfactory lighting conditions are achieved when the fitting is installed and recessed into the wall at approximately one metre from floor level. Possible glare is avoided by shielding the bulb, Fig. 99. Normal lighting is required for cleaning the sauna, and variable lighting can be used to serve different requirements. General lighting regulations and instructions are followed in the dressing and washing rooms.

Local regulations must be followed when installing light fittings.

Electrical Installations

Local regulations must be followed, and the person responsible for the design, construction, repair and maintenance of electrical fittings and equipment must be duly authorized.

Selection of the electric stove type

The installation instructions delivered with the electric stove list the minimum and maximum permissible volume of the stove room according to stove size and output. These instructions also contain information on the space required by the stove, protective distances from other materials, and electrical installations. Electric stoves and the required distances from other components are discussed in Chapter 5.

The type of stove depends on the number of bathers, the average duration of the bath, ventilation, thermal insulation, and the possible presence of uninsulated walls and ceilings.

In saunas under 10 m³ in volume, a stove of 1 kW/m³ output is usually selected. Larger stove rooms permit a lower ratio of output to volume, e.g. 0.7 kW/m³. This requires that there are no uninsulated wall or ceiling surfaces and that the window is not larger than 0.5 m². If there are brick or concrete surfaces in the stove room, 1.5 m³ must be added to dimensioning per each square metre of these surfaces.

Space requirements of an electric stove

The electric stove must be installed according to the manufacturer's instructions. The space required depends on the dimensions of the stove and the required distances from inflammable materials. If the control device forms an integral part, the stove is installed so as to leave the controls visible on the unobstructed side of the stove and to permit easy use. An unrestricted area in front of the controls can be for example 800 mm. The height of the stove room must also be taken into account as specified in the instructions pertaining to the stove.

Mounting the electric stove

Stove mounted on the wall require, for example, a sufficiently large and strong length of boarding within the wall component to which the mounting screws can be affixed. The weight of the stove and the stones must be taken into account. Electric stoves installed on the floor must be fixed in place.

Tubing and connection boxes

The required connection boxes and installation tubing for the cable are to be placed near the electric stove. The connection box is installed at a maximum height of 300 mm from floor level next to the location where the stove is fixed in place.

In the walls and ceilings, the tubing is usually placed on the warm side of the thermal insulation, but in saunas outside the thermal insulation of the stove room. Special care must be taken not to place the tubing within the thermal insulation.

Controls and protective devices

The control and safety devices of electric stoves are particular to each model. The type designations of various control units and thermostat-limiter devices are given in the installation instructions of the stove. When choosing the stove model it should already be taken into account whether it will be controlled from outside the stove room, with a timer, or switched on prior to each bath.

A separate control unit may not be placed in the stove room, and it can be installed in the washing room only if it is drop- and splash-proof (grade IP 21 or IP 34 depending on classification).

Installing a boiler

The water boiler should primarily be placed in a dry room. If it has to be installed in the stove room or washing room, the requirements of cleaning must be taken into account.

Installing a boiler in the stove room

According to current regulations only splash-proof electrical appliances can be installed in the sauna. As long as the device is less than 1 metre from floor level no heat resistance requirements are placed on the boiler. A further requirement is that the manufacturer specifi-

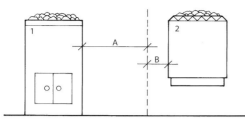

Fig. 104. Installation of a wood-fired (1) and an electric (2) stove next to each other without a protective barrier.

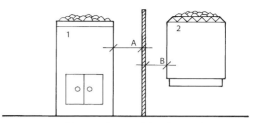

Fig. 105. Installation of a wood-fired (1) and an electric (2) stove next to each other with a protective barrier between them.

cally intended the boiler to be used in a sauna. An 800 mm area must be left free in front of the controls of the boiler.

Installation in the washing room

The casing of a water boiler which is to be installed in a washing or shower room must be of drip- or splash-proof construction (mainly grades IP 21 or IP 34).

Electric heating outside bathing hours

Electric heaters for sauna rooms must have splash-proof grade casings. In the sauna, the heater is located under the platforms, with a connection box and tubing for the leads at 300 mm from floor level. The required casing grade in other rooms depends on their use (washing room, shower, dressing room, pool area).

The design of the floor heating element cables proceeds from specific heat requirements and electrical safety regulations. The instructions of the manufacturer of the heating cable are to be followed carefully in the installation, handling, placing and fixing of the cables.

In the floor, the heating element cable is usually encased in a concrete slab. In designing the heating, special attention must be paid to heat loss through the foundation of the building.

In view of the thermal insulation properties of the floor surface and the desired surface temperature, the heating cable is placed so to provide as even a surface temperature as possible.

It is not permitted to install a heating cable in the floor beneath an electric stove fixed in place.

Installing an Electric Stove and a Wood-fired Stove in the Same Sauna

If required, it is possible to install both an electric and a wood-fired stove in the same stove room. Each stove is to be installed according to specific instructions. The installation of stoves and the required safety limits are also discussed in Chapter 5. Local safety regulations must be followed when installing stoves.

The distance between the stoves must be the sum of their respective protective distances, Fig. 104. The minimum distance can be reduced with a protective barrier, preventing the radiation of heat from one stove to another, Fig. 105. A light barrier is suitable for this purpose. Such a barrier can be made of stiff mineral board (minimum thickness 7 mm), or non-corrosive sheet metal 1 mm thick. The barrier must extend to at least the height of the upper edge of the electric stove, but no more than 200 mm above it. Towards the sides the barrier must extend so far as to prevent direct radiation of heat between the stoves. The minimum distance of an electric stove from the protective barrier must be according to the installation instructions. A wood-fired stove must be placed at a minimum distance of 250 mm from a single light barrier, and 125 mm from a double barrier (30 mm ventilation gap to be left between the boards).

The only electrical device permitted near the wood-fired stove is the sensing device of the thermostat or limiting device serving the electric stove. This can be installed anywhere between the floor and ceiling at a lateral distance of 400 mm from the uninsulated stove. The sensing device of the electric stove must be placed on the other side of it than the wood-fired stove, or it is installed at the location of the electric stove as stated in the installation instructions.

Simultaneous use of the stoves is not allowed. This should be specifically mentioned in the instructions for the electric stove and also on a sign or plaque placed in a visible location.

The heat of the wood-fired stove may activate the limiting device of the electric stove. Accordingly, the limiting device should be of a type that can be reset by hand.

When planning the sauna, it is necessary to ask the stove manufacturer's opinion concerning the installation described in this section.

7. Smoke Saunas

This chapter is on the construction of traditional and modern smoke saunas. There are also instructions on the dimensioning of smoke stoves, their locations, protective distances from other materials, and instructions on the construction of a smoke stove of brick and masonry.

General Remarks

The builder of a smoke sauna is best instructed to rely on old tradition as much as possible. However, the main properties of the smoke sauna can also be achieved with slightly non-traditional means.

Smoke saunas are also discussed in Chapter 1. The smoke stove is presented in Chapter 5.

The location of the smoke sauna

The smoke sauna is normally located apart from other buildings at a minimum distance of 20 metres from them.

If it is necessary to locate the smoke sauna in another building, it is necessary to consult local fire and building inspection authorities already in the planning stage. A fire-proof wall (a partitioning wall is not sufficient) is usually built between the smoke sauna and the adjoining rooms. A smoke sauna should not be installed in a building for lodging guests.

Constructing a Traditional Smoke Sauna

Until the turn of the century, a number of considerably different sauna types were in use in various parts of Finland.

The traditional smoke sauna can be designed according to two different principles.

In the traditional method the builder follows ethnographically researched techniques and solutions. Accordingly, the choice of sauna will depend on regional types, historical stages and methods of construction. Saunas of this type can be built, for example, at holiday homes and tourist centres.

Further information on the design of traditional smoke saunas is found in ethnographic studies and literature, existing old smoke saunas, local museums, and the Muurame Sauna Museum with traditional saunas from different parts of Finland.

Using the modern method, the properties of the smoke sauna are achieved with the means of contemporary structural and architectural design.

The traditional method

It is possible to select a smoke sauna type of a certain age with accordingly defined methods of construction, materials and features of architecture. The type and age also dictate the details of the platforms, stoves, doors, windows and fittings. A design of coherent style requires care in executing the details.

Fig. 106. Smoke sauna. Muurame Sauna Museum. Photo: Teemu Töyrylä.

The foundation

Smoke saunas for summer use are usually built on corner-stone foundations. The gap between the bottom log and the ground is filled with stones. The spaces between the stones ensure ventilation and help to keep the bottom log dry.

The drains of the sauna are discussed in Chapter 6.

Log types and corner joints

The main chronological characteristics of saunas are the log types and specific corner-joining techniques.

A diagonally notched joint (Fig. 107) was commonly used when the axe was the only available tool. It could easily be used for making diagonal surfaces and corner joints.

The straight-notched joint came into use through the spread of carving axes and saws. Most of the log building erected in Finland in the 19th and 20th centuries were made with this technique. The logs were first notched with a special axe and then finished in situ. See Fig. 108.

Fish-tail and other complex joining methods are mainly 20th-century developments. These were mostly used in saunas in the 1920s and '30s. These methods conserve timber, but require great skill and precision.

Round-notched corners with the notch on one side are mainly an eastern (East Karelian) tradition. In Eastern Karelia the notch was made on the upper surface of the log (Fig. 109 a), while in Finland the notch was always on the bottom surface, Fig. 109 b. At present, this type of joint is used in the serial production of logs.

Floor and ceiling

Initially, the smoke saunas had only earth floors. Later, flat stones, individual planks and poles were used. In time, floors of boarding were also built.

The oldest roof types are of birch-bark, poles, turf, beams, boarding and straw construction.

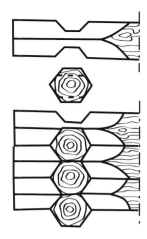

Fig. 107. Diagonally notched joint.

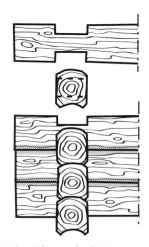

Fig. 108. Straight-notched joint.

Fig. 109. Round-notched corner joints a) East Karelian b) Finnish.

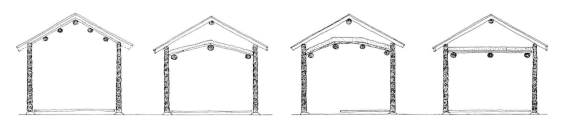

Fig. 110. Development of roof and ceiling structures in the smoke sauna. Drawing: Risto Vuolle-Apiala.

SMOKE SAUNAS

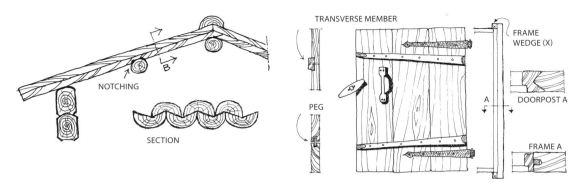

Fig. 111. Roof construction.
Drawing: Risto Vuolle-Apiala.

Fig. 112. The door of a smoke sauna.
Drawing: Risto Vuolle-Apiala.

Shingled roofs did not become common until the late 19th century. Figs. 111 and 113 show different types of ceilings and roofs in smoke saunas.

A combined roof and ceiling was used in the old type of sauna. The shape of the interior roof surface has been influenced by the roofing material and technical developments. The form of the ceiling was dictated by the specific use of the sauna and the location of the platforms. Later, the ceiling became a completely separate component.

Doors and windows

The windows of the sauna developed from small vents, approximately the height of a log, with wooden shutters into four-paned windows. The window is installed in the wall in the location hewn from the outside.

An unhewn log is left below the door of the sauna. The upper part of the door stands ca. 120–140 mm from floor level. The door is ca. 750–900 mm wide, and is made of three or four boards joined with wedged frames, Fig. 112.

The modern method

A traditional smoke sauna can also be built by selecting the main features of local traditions, which are then executed in modern techniques, e.g. with industrially produced logs and modern insulating and roofing materials. The traditional smoke saunas were simple structures, and the presently common ornaments or specially shaped log corners were not used.

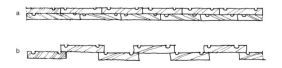

Fig. 113. Roofs of boarding.
Drawing: Risto Vuolle-Apiala.

Building a Modern Smoke Sauna

The planning and design of a modern smoke sauna proceeds from general considerations concerning the quality of the hot vapour, the use of the sauna, and building methods. Requirements concerning the quality of the hot vapour and the bathing conditions can be met by following a few basic principles.

The size of the sauna
The size of the sauna depends on the number of people using at one time. The most suitable size for traditional family saunas is 9 m³. The reason for this is that the smoke stove is larger than a normal sauna stove and separate areas are required for the platforms, water containers and washing.

The height of the stove room
The interior height of the sauna should meet the so-called Pälsi's Law, according to which the bather must be seated with his or her whole body (including the feet) above the stove stones. This ensures even and sufficient heat from head to toe, Fig. 114.

The smoke level
During the heating, a buffer of smoke forms above the level of the top stones on the stove. The window should be placed below this level to prevent it from becoming sooty, Fig. 118.

Interior furnishings
The interior components and furnishings should primarily be of high-quality timber. Timber with high resin content, such as knotty pine, should be avoided. Chapter 3 on the design and planning of the components of the sauna lists the properties of suitable timbers.

The interior of the smoke sauna should conform to the building as a whole. Shown in Fig. 115 is an example of a platform for a smoke sauna.

Fig. 114. Pälsi's Law. The bather must be seated completely above the stones of the stove.

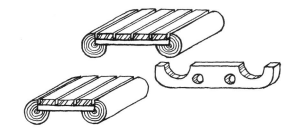

Fig. 115. An example of a platform of aspen with removable seat parts.

Fig. 116. Smoke sauna under construction with traditional methods. Design and Photograph by Risto Vuolle-Apiala.

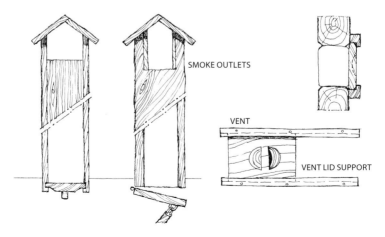

Fig. 117. Vents in a smoke sauna. Drawing: Risto Vuolle-Apiala.

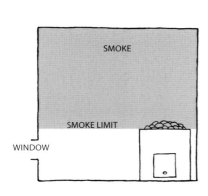
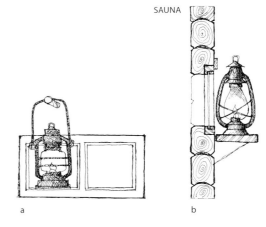

Fig. 118. The location of the window in a smoke sauna.

Fig. 119. Lighting for a smoke sauna. a) window between the stove room and the entrance with a lantern hanging from a peg, b) lantern on a small ledge.

Fire-safety considerations

Special attention must be paid to fire safety in a smoke sauna. This is particularly important if this type of sauna is constructed within another building. The section on the shielding of the stove lists the required distances between the stove and other materials.

The following fire-safety aspects must also be taken into account:

1. No outlet should be placed above the stove. During the heating an outlet above the stove will act like a flue and will easily catch fire.

2. The ceiling must be built to a tight fit to prevent even the smallest gaps that might cause draughts.

3. Local fire authorities should be consulted before applying for permission to build a smoke sauna.

Ventilation

The ventilation should be arranged as in traditional saunas. This means a generous supply of fresh air into the lower part of the stove room and an outlet at a high location in the wall or leading via the ceiling through the roof, Fig. 117. The ventilation of saunas is discussed in Chapter 6.

Lighting

The lighting of smoke saunas is traditionally an uncomplicated matter. A lantern or other source of light can be placed outside the window or in the lower part of the stove room, Fig. 119. Darkness is usually felt to be a pleasant aspect of the mood of the sauna.

Electric light fittings must not be installed higher than 1 metre from floor level in a smoke sauna. The casing of a light fitting placed higher than 0.5 m must be of grade IP 65, and a fitting at a maximum height of 0.5 m must have a casing of grade IP 54 (minimum).

The Smoke Stove

An essential feature of the smoke stove is that the smoke is let into the sauna during the heating. The heating is discussed in further detail below. Different types of smoke stoves are shown in Fig. 120.

The dimensioning of the stove proceeds from the size of the sauna, the required bathing time, the stove type, and the amount of stones.

The East Finnish type with unfixed stones requires approximately 1,100 litres of stones, corresponding to ca. 60 l per cubic metre and some 150 l per bather. If the stove has a masonry or brickwork framework or is completely encased or fitted with a lid, a small amount of stones is required.

The stove stones should withstand high temperatures, as the lower part of the stove has to be heated to a red glow. Among the best types of rock for these purposes are olivine and peridotite. The stones should not exude sulphur or other impurities.

Factory-made smoke stoves are also available. An electric stove must not be installed in a smoke sauna. Smoke stoves are also discussed in Chapter 5.

The location of the stove

The stove must be located so as to make it as easy as possible to tend the fire. The stove can be placed:
- completely in the stove room
- with the fire and ash chamber opening onto an adjacent room, e.g. an entrance, washing or dressing room, from where the heating takes place. To ensure ventilation, an opening must be made in the fire chamber on the stove room side.

Fig. 121. Smoke stoves. a) open stove, b) brick stove open on top to which a lid can be added, c) stove encased in brickwork. Drawing: Risto Vuolle-Apiala.

- with the stove partly sunk into the floor. Accordingly, the fire and ash chamber are in a separate space on a lower elevation, and the fire will be tended from a cellar or from outside the sauna.

The foundation of the stove

As a flueless fireplace construction, the smoke stove can be placed in a separate concrete slab of sufficient durability. The slab must be paced on a gravel layer at least 200 mm thick, or on some other immobile foundation not affected by the freezing of the ground.

Protective measures

There are no detailed instructions on the protection of smoke stoves and the required distances from other materials. In view of fire safety, a brick stove is safer than an open stove. The required distances between an open stove and other components must be defined separately. Existing regulations can be followed in the case of brick stoves.

The sides of a brick stove must be at least 50 mm (horizontally) from inflammable materials. A distance of 500 mm is required in front of the fire chamber opening. For safety reasons an interior door can also be installed in the fire chamber.

The stove stones must be 1000 mm (horizontally) apart from other components. This distance can be reduced by 50% when using a single light barrier and by 75% when using a double light barrier.

A single light barrier can be made from non-inflammable fibre-reinforced cement board (minimum thickness 7 mm) or hot galvanized sheet metal (minimum thickness 1 mm). A double barrier can be made from two of the above.

The protective boards are affixed to their sup-

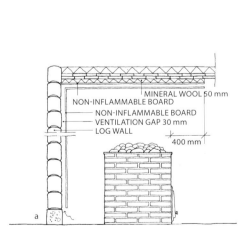
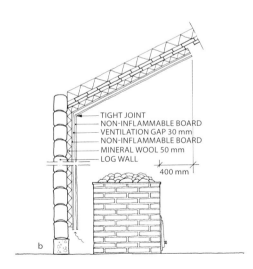

Fig. 121. Protective measures.

SMOKE SAUNAS | 99

ports and where necessary to each other with screws. A ventilation gap of at least 30 mm must be left between the barrier and the protected surface, for example by using bushings. The installation of a light protective barrier is described in Chapter 5.

In a smoke sauna the ceiling above the stove must always be protected. A single light barrier is sufficient if the distance from the stones to the ceiling is more than 1500 mm. A 50 mm layer of non-inflammable mineral wool is placed above the barrier.

If the distance is less than 1500 mm (minimum 1000 mm), a double light barrier must be used, also backed by a 50 mm layer of non-inflammable mineral wool. The protective barriers are extended to at least 400 mm from the smoke stove, Fig. 121. If only the ceiling is protected, the barrier should extend to the wall behind the stove.

RT stove types

Presented in this chapter are two smoke stove models of different size: RT 91-10483 (770) and RT 91-10483 (910).

The numbers in brackets indicate the height (k) of the top course of bricks from floor level.

The lower model (770) can be used in saunas

Table 10. Dimensions of the RT-model stoves

	Type (k) 770	Type (k) 910
Height of stone layer	ca. 300 mm	ca. 400 mm
Height of fire chamber	420 mm	480 mm

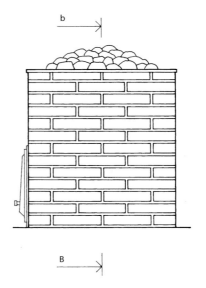

Fig. 122. RT-type stove. Scale 1:20.

designed for baths of 1.5–2 hours and the higher stove for baths of 2.0–3.0 hours. The thermal output can be increased by adding depth to the stove. Bathing times can be lengthened by installing a lid over the stones. The dimensions of the stoves are given in Table 10.

Materials and equipment

Bricks

The dimensions of the flue bricks are 257 x 123 x 57 mm. The bricks must be selected, well-fired, even-sized, regular in shape, intact and of even colour. The fire-proof bricks are of the same size as the flue bricks.

The lower stove model (770) requires 115 flue bricks and 55 fire-proof bricks. The larger model (910) requires 135 flue bricks and 60 fire-proof bricks.

Mortar

The smoke stove is built with mortar consisting of loam mortar and masonry cement in equal parts.

If there is a risk of freezing owing to moisture and cold conditions, only masonry cement should be used.

The fire-proof bricks are laid with fire-proof mortar. One hundred kilograms of mortar and 18 kg of fire-proof mortar are needed.

The stones

Peridotite is one of several suitable rock types for the smoke stove. The stones must be of different size, varying between 50 and 150 mm. The stove can be made more effective by using larger stones. Stove stones are discussed in more detail in Chapter 5.

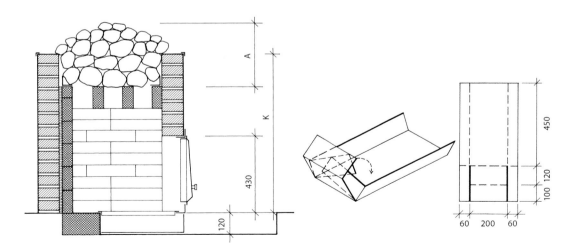

Fig. 123. RT-type stove. Section A. Scale 1:20.

Fig. 124. Ash pan. Measurements in millimetres.

The grate

The grate is of cast iron, either with or without a framework. The masonry dimensions are: width 140 mm, depth 390 mm. The framework is 210 mm wide and 410 mm deep.

The stove door

The masonry dimensions for the cast-iron stove door are 270 x 340 mm.

The ash pan

The ash pan is made of 1 mm sheet steel as shown in Fig. 124.

Reinforcing the stove

The upper edge of the brickwork outside casing is reinforced with L-section steel (20 mm x 20 mm x 3 mm) welded into a frame.

Angle steel bars

Installed beneath the stove door is an angle steel bar 70 mm high, e.g. 50 mm wide, and 500 mm long. Above the door is a 50 x 50 mm angle steel bar 330 mm long.

The construction of the stove

The size of the grate must be taken into account when the base of the stove is cast or made of bricks.

The outer casing is made of flue bricks with 10–13 mm pointing. The pointing of the fire chamber is ca. 2–4 mm. Owing to thermal expansion, the fire chamber is separated from the body of the stove with a 5–10 mm expansion joint filled with non-inflammable fibre.

The stove stones are laid so that the lowermost (ca. 100–150 mm) stones are placed on the brick supports leaving the gaps as open as possible. These stones are then overlaid with 80–100 mm stones, followed by a top layer of ca. 50–70 mm stones.

Heating a Smoke Sauna

The general principles of heating a smoke sauna are presented in the following. Each sauna is a unique construction and its heating technique must be learned separately.

There are highly different views on the type of firewood. Alder is the only species accepted by all experts. In some parts of Finland, spruce is regarded as good firewood for smoke stoves. Birch with large amounts of bark has been avoided because it produces soot, while aspen burns slowly.

Care is required in heating the smoke sauna, and for safety reasons the person responsible should remain near the sauna throughout the heating. A smoke sauna can be equipped with a proper fire extinguisher. The stove must be heated to produce a red glow in part of the stone layer. This is usually achieved by filling the chamber twice with firewood. The burning takes approximately two hours. After the heating, the coals and ashes are raked properly, and water can be thrown on the stones to get rid of soot. The smoke outlet and the doors can then be closed.

The time available for use varies according to the size of the sauna and the structure of the stove. With an open stove, it was possible to begin bathing immediately after the firewood and coals had burnt. A brick-casing stove with the door closed preserves heat better than an open stove, permitting 1–3 hours of use.

The sauna must also be prepared for the bathers. The first thing to do is to throw water on the stones to wash out loose soot and ashes. The platforms, benches and floor are then cleaned, and the washing water is brought in. The sauna must also be properly aired at this stage.

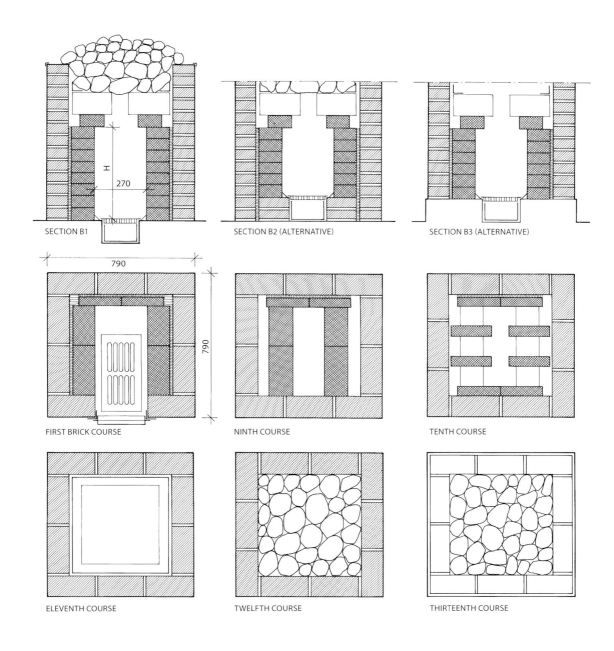

Fig. 125. Sections of the RT-type stove. Scale 1:20.

Rakennustieto | Building Information

Building Information is the leading provider of construction information in Finland.
The Building Information Foundation RTS (Rakennustietosäätiö) is a private, non-profit foundation whose task is to promote good town planning and building practices as well as sound property management principles. The Building Information Foundation RTS is the parent entity of Building Information and acts as the entire organisation's research and development unit. Projects that are developed into profitable independent businesses are transferred from the non-profit Foundation to its operative company.

Building Information Ltd implements the Building Information Foundation RTS's mission by producing and selling products and services that enable construction and property professionals and consumers to daily comply with good planning, construction and property management practices.

The RT File compiles the most important standards, regulations and building products regarding the design and construction of buildings. It is intended for architects, structural engineers and builders for daily use.

Rakennustieto Publishing

Our publications in Finnish provide instructions for good design and building practices, aiming at solutions that are technically correct, cost-conscious implementation and guidelines that are in accordance with the law. In addition to books in Finnish, we also publish English-language architectural books for international markets. Rakennustieto is a unique publishing house, as it is the only Finnish publisher and worldwide distributor in the field of architecture. We want to spread information about our books on architecture, Finnish architects and Finnish design among readers worldwide.
www. rakennustieto.fi/publishing

Online bookshop

Books are easy to order through our online shop **http://kauppa.rakennustieto.fi**. Orders can be made also through our customer service, phone +358 207 476 401,
Rakennustieto Oy (Building Information Ltd), PO. Box 1004, 00101 Helsinki, Finland.

www. rakennustieto.fi

Contemporary Finnish Saunas

 A Yard Sauna

 The Sireenimäki Sauna

 The Thorsby Smoke Sauna

A Yard Sauna

The building is located in the back yard of the so-called Merchant's Quarter of the Suomenlinna island fortification off Helsinki – a classified World Heritage Site. There are two existing houses on the small plot. The new, distinctly modern yard building was built in 2000 on the site of a demolished shed.

The appearance of the sauna strived for the lightness of a traditional outbuilding; the depth of the building frame is narrow and the building was laid on foundation columns such that it does not touch the ground, again adding to the feeling of lightness. The 20 square metres of floor area includes a sauna, dressing room and woodworking workroom.

The exterior is clad with sealed white-painted broad pine boards, with louvered panels of transparently-varnished, dense-grain Lapland pine. The wood-fired sauna stove is backed by awall of large soapstone slabs.

Architect Seppo Häkli

The dressing-room window, partly glazed with Japanese paper, looks out on to its own back yard. The door on the right leads to the sitting area. The floor is oiled, heat-treated birch, while all other interior surfaces are untreated alder.

The back yard sauna has a partial view of the passage between the two dwellings on the site.

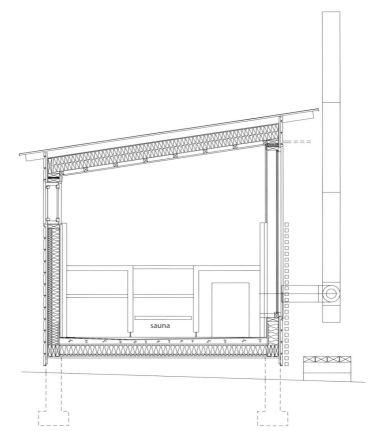

Section 1:50

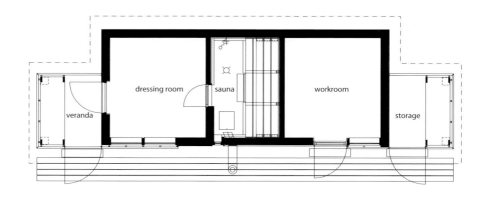

Plan 1:100

108 | CONTEMPORARY FINNISH SAUNAS

Jussi Tiainen

The sauna has traditional plank benches. The soapstone stove has a matt finish.

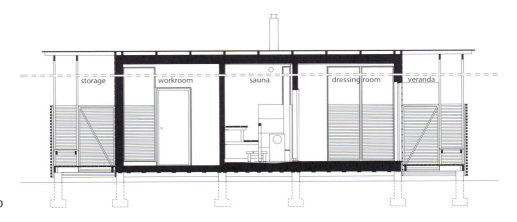

Section 1:100

CONTEMPORARY FINNISH SAUNAS

The Sireenimäki Sauna

The entrance facade of the Sireenimäki Sauna has the feeling of a Japanese farmhouse, with its large roof and terrace lined with columns made from slender tree trunks. The plank boarding and the solid rear facade refers to a barn, which is a traditional feature in the Finnish landscape of cultivated fields.

Various building techniques have been used in the different spaces of the sauna. Either side of the masonry construction washing room in the centre of the building are sections built in wood, one containing the hot room and the other a lounge filled with natural light. In each room the dimensions – including the height – were selected to best serve the use of the space. The wide roof, supported by columns, shelters the spacious outside terrace as well as the delicate detailing of the windows and doors. The wood plank roof protects the layer of bitumen felt against UV radiation and mechanical wear. Under the roof is an open attic space.

The opposite benches in the hot room are placed so that they form steps. The floor of the sauna consists of only wooden planks, and the benches are not supported on the wooden floor. The sauna has a heat-retaining wood-heated stove. The floor in the washing room rests directly on the ground and includes under-floor heating. The changing room has a ventilated crawl space.

Architect Marko Huttunen

Various building techniques have been used in the different spaces of the sauna.

The entrance facade.

The wide roof shelters the spacious terrace.

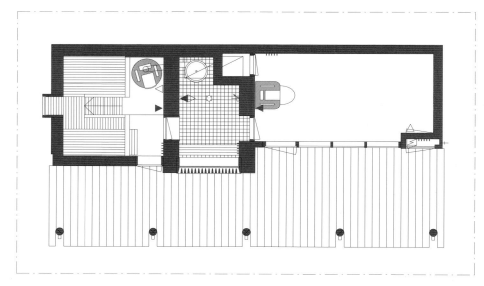

Plan 1:100

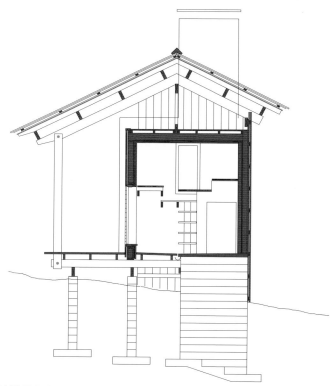

Section 1:100

Mikko Mälkki

The opposite benches are placed so that they form steps.

The Thorsby Smoke Sauna

This smoke sauna, built in 1997, is really a bathing complex, with a hot room, a cold pool, and an air bath. There is nothing in the building that is not visible or that cannot be experienced directly.

This "sauna machine" is intended to transfer thermal energy to people as pleasantly as possible. The low massive stove in the tall room ensures an even distribution of heat over the bather's entire body.

The firing of the stove from outside, the leading of the smoke directly into the room and out through the smoke-hatch, the ventilation through the door, the cooling down outside, and the washing water flowing out through the floor all help to create a natural relationship between the indoors and outdoors.

Architect Marko Huttunen

Mikko Mälkki

The sauna soon after its completion in 1997.

Marko Huttunen

By 2005 the wooden facades of the sauna have been turned grey by the weathering process as well as blackened by us

The Sauna is divided vertically in to hot-steam and washing sections.

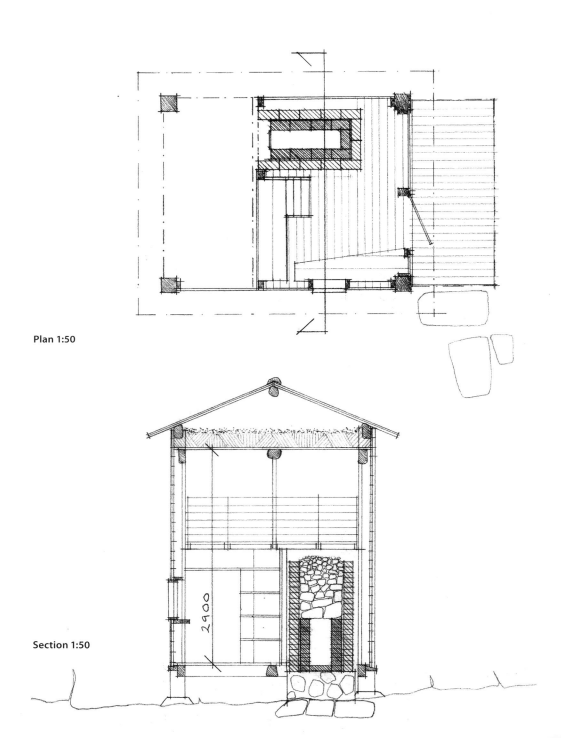

Plan 1:50

Section 1:50

THE DOOR, DETAIL DRAWING

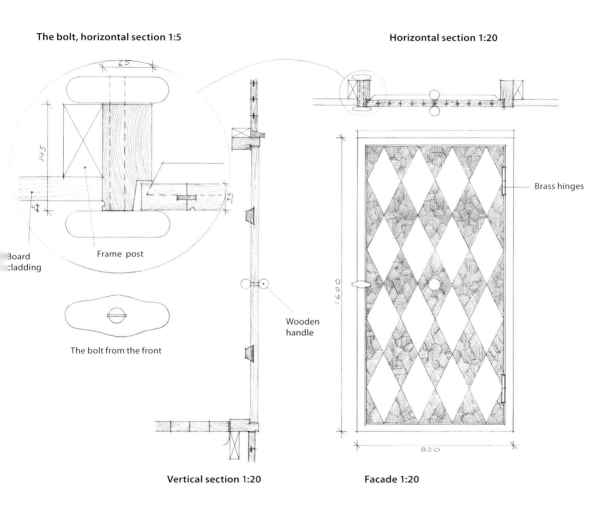

Rakennustieto Publishing – Books on Architecture

Villas and Saunas in Finland

Harri Hautajärvi

This book presents summer villas and saunas in Finland, from the marine archipelago via lake district to the fells of the north – a total of 44 individually-designed buildings that represent the best of recent Finnish summer home and sauna architecture.

ISBN 978-951-682-780-6
hardback

Small Houses in Finland

Esa Piironen (ed.)

The book presents a selection of the best single-family houses in Finland from the last twenty-five years. Each of the 29 houses presented shows a different approach to the design of a small house.

2nd edition, 2007, 128 pp | ISBN 978-951-682-751-6 | hardback

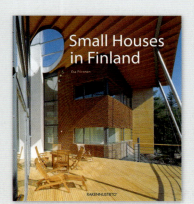

Office Buildings in Finland

The Association of Finnish Architects' Offices ATL

The book aspires to create a wide perspective on the various trends in current Finnish office architecture. If the contents of the book had to be summed up in a few words, it would be "humane high-technology".

2007, 167 pp
ISBN 978-751-682-808-7
softback

Alvar Aalto Apartments

Photographs Jari Jetsonen, Text Sirkkaliisa Jetsonen
Article Markku Lahti, Forewords Peter Reed

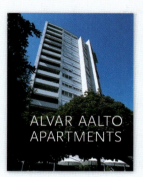

The book presents ten apartment blocks and two student dormitories by Aalto built in Finland, Sweden, Germany, Switzerland and the United States, from the 1920s to the end of the 1960s.

2004, 160 pp
ISBN 951-682-732-2
softback

Alvar Aalto Houses

Photographs Jari Jetsonen, Text Markku Lahti
Article Sirkkaliisa Jetsonen, Foreword Hiroshi Naito

The book presents eight single-family houses by Aalto from 1920s to the end of the 1960s, built in Finland, Estonia and France. Among them are Villa Tammekann in Tartu, Estonia, Villa Mairea in Noormarkku, Finland and Maison Louis Carré in Bazoches-sur-Guyonne, France.

2005, 160 pp
ISBN 951-682-775-6
softback

Zumthor – Spirit of Nature Wood Architecture Award 2006

This book presents three projects by Peter Zumthor: Haus Luzi, realised in 2002, and Haus Annalisa and Pension Briol which are still plans. These are featured with beautiful watercolour sketches, and models and plans, which give a good idea of the designing process.

2nd edition 2007, 80 pp
ISBN 978-951-682-807-0
softback

www.rakennustieto.fi/publishing

Books are easy to order through our online shop http://kauppa.rakennustieto.fi. Orders can be made also through our customer service, phone +358 207 476 401, Rakennustieto Oy, PO. Box 1004, 00101 Helsinki, Finland.